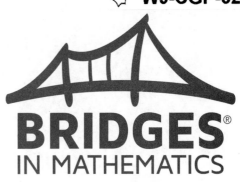

BRIDGES®
IN MATHEMATICS

SECOND EDITION
HOME CONNECTIONS

GRADE
2

Published by The MATH LEARNING CENTER *Salem, Oregon*

W9-CGP-325

Bridges in Mathematics Second Edition Grade 2 Home Connections

The Bridges in Mathematics Grade 2 package consists of:

Bridges in Mathematics Grade 2 Teachers Guide Units 1–8

Bridges in Mathematics Grade 2 Assessment Guide

Bridges in Mathematics Grade 2 Teacher Masters

Bridges in Mathematics Grade 2 Student Book

Bridges in Mathematics Grade 2 Home Connections

Bridges in Mathematics Grade 2 Teacher Masters Answer Key

Bridges in Mathematics Grade 2 Student Book Answer Key

Bridges in Mathematics Grade 2 Home Connections Answer Key

Bridges in Mathematics Grade 2 Components & Manipulatives

Bridges Educator Site

Work Place Games & Activities

Number Corner Grade 2 Teachers Guide Volumes 1–3

Number Corner Grade 2 Teacher Masters

Number Corner Grade 2 Student Book

Number Corner Grade 2 Teacher Masters Answer Key

Number Corner Grade 2 Student Book Answer Key

Number Corner Grade 2 Components & Manipulatives

Word Resource Cards

Digital resources noted in italics.

The Math Learning Center, PO Box 12929, Salem, Oregon 97309. Tel 1 (800) 575-8130
www.mathlearningcenter.org

Prepared for publication using Mac OS X and Adobe Creative Suite.
Printed in the United States of America.

To reorder Home Connections, refer to number 2B2HC5 (package of 5 sets).

QBB2903
06012020_LSC
Updated 2019-01-01.

Bridges in Mathematics is a standards-based K–5 curriculum that provides a unique blend of concept development and skills practice in the context of problem solving. It incorporates Number Corner, a collection of daily skill-building activities for students.

The Math Learning Center is a nonprofit organization serving the education community. Our mission is to inspire and enable individuals to discover and develop their mathematical confidence and ability. We offer innovative and standards-based professional development, curriculum, materials, and resources to support learning and teaching. To find out more, visit us at www.mathlearningcenter.org.

ISBN 978-1-60262-346-0

Bridges Grade 2
Home Connections

Unit 1
Figure the Facts

Unit 2
Place Value & Measurement with Jack's Beanstalks

Unit 3
Addition & Subtraction Within One Hundred

Unit 4
Measurement

Unit 5
Place Value to One Thousand

Unit 6
Geometry

Unit 7
Measurement, Fractions & Multi-Digit Computation with Hungry Ants

Unit 8
Measurement, Data & Multi-Digit Computation with Marble Rolls

🏠 Numbers & Shapes page 1 of 2

1 Trace the words and numbers. Then draw a line to the matching set.

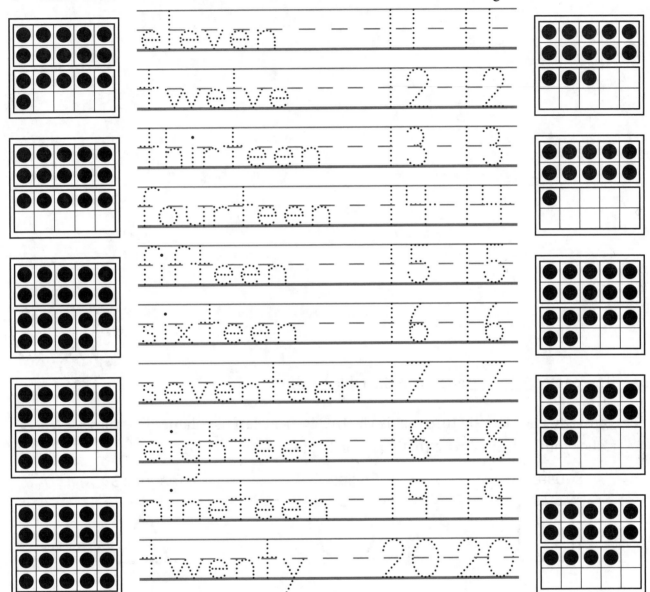

eleven	11 - 11	
twelve	12 - 12	
thirteen	13 - 13	
fourteen	14 - 14	
fifteen	15 - 15	
sixteen	16 - 16	
seventeen	17 - 17	
eighteen	18 - 18	
nineteen	19 - 19	
twenty	20 - 20	

2 Fill in the missing numbers on the line below.

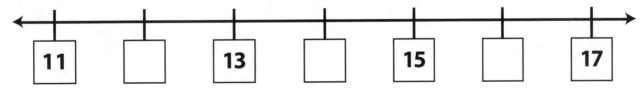

| 11 | | 13 | | 15 | | 17 |

(continued on next page)

Numbers & Shapes page 2 of 2

3 There were 3 apples on the table. Jan put 6 more apples on the table. How many apples were on the table in all? Show your work.

There were _____ apples on the table in all.

4 **CHALLENGE** Make a picture that is worth 24¢. You can use shapes like these. Label your picture. Prove that it is worth 24¢.

Square: 5¢   Circle: 4¢   Triangle: 3¢

Addition & Subtraction Practice page 1 of 2

1 Add. Count the dots to help.

$\begin{array}{r} 5 \\ + 0 \\ \hline 5 \end{array}$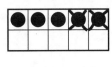

$\begin{array}{r} 4 \\ + 2 \\ \hline \end{array}$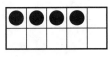

$\begin{array}{r} 3 \\ + 2 \\ \hline \end{array}$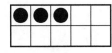

$\begin{array}{r} 6 \\ + 1 \\ \hline \end{array}$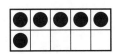

$\begin{array}{r} 3 \\ + 0 \\ \hline \end{array}$

$\begin{array}{r} 2 \\ + 2 \\ \hline \end{array}$

$\begin{array}{r} 1 \\ + 4 \\ \hline \end{array}$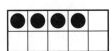

$\begin{array}{r} 2 \\ + 5 \\ \hline \end{array}$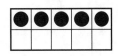

$\begin{array}{r} 1 \\ + 5 \\ \hline \end{array}$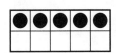

$\begin{array}{r} 0 \\ + 6 \\ \hline \end{array}$

$\begin{array}{r} 3 \\ + 1 \\ \hline \end{array}$

$\begin{array}{r} 6 \\ + 2 \\ \hline \end{array}$

2 Subtract. Cross out the dots to help.

$\begin{array}{r} 5 \\ - 2 \\ \hline 3 \end{array}$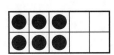

$\begin{array}{r} 4 \\ - 2 \\ \hline \end{array}$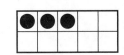

$\begin{array}{r} 3 \\ - 2 \\ \hline \end{array}$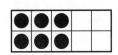

$\begin{array}{r} 6 \\ - 1 \\ \hline \end{array}$

$\begin{array}{r} 3 \\ - 0 \\ \hline \end{array}$

$\begin{array}{r} 2 \\ - 2 \\ \hline \end{array}$

$\begin{array}{r} 4 \\ - 1 \\ \hline \end{array}$

$\begin{array}{r} 5 \\ - 0 \\ \hline \end{array}$

$\begin{array}{r} 5 \\ - 1 \\ \hline \end{array}$

$\begin{array}{r} 6 \\ - 0 \\ \hline \end{array}$

$\begin{array}{r} 3 \\ - 1 \\ \hline \end{array}$

$\begin{array}{r} 6 \\ - 2 \\ \hline \end{array}$

(continued on next page)

© The Math Learning Center | mathlearningcenter.org

NAME _____ | DATE _____

Addition & Subtraction Practice page 2 of 2

3 Marco has 6 dollars. How many more dollars does he need to have 10 dollars in all? Show your work.

Marco needs _____ dollars to have 10 dollars in all.

4 **CHALLENGE** Katy has 5 dollars. How many more *dimes* does she need to have 8 dollars in all? Show your work.

Katy needs _____ more dimes to have 8 dollars in all.

NAME | **DATE**

 Doubles & More page 1 of 2

1 Add.

0	0	1
+ 0	+ 1	+ 1

1	2	2
+ 2	+ 2	+ 3

3	3	4
+ 3	+ 4	+ 4

4	5	10
+ 5	+ 5	+ 10

2 Find the sums. Make dots in the frames to show the answers.

4 + 3 = ___7___   3 + 2 = _____   5 + 4 = _____

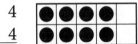

4 + 4 = _____   4 + 3 = _____   5 + 5 = _____

2 + 3 = _____   4 + 5 = _____   2 + 2 = _____

(continued on next page)

Doubles & More page 2 of 2

3 Gus had some fish. He got 6 more fish at the pet store. Now he has 11 fish. How many fish did Gus have to start with? Show your work.

Gus started out with _____ fish.

4 **CHALLENGE** Mrs. Jones has ducks and sheep on her farm. The animals have a total of 6 heads and 16 legs. How many ducks does Mrs. Jones have? How many sheep does Mrs. Jones have? Show your work.

Mrs. Jones has _____ ducks and _____ sheep.

Thinking About Fives page 1 of 8

Note to Families

This assignment includes a game we just learned in class and a worksheet that provides more practice counting by, adding, and subtracting 5s. Read the game instructions with your child, cut out the cards, and play the game several times. Then have your child complete the worksheet and return it to school.

Materials

- Thinking About Fives pages 1–8
- paperclip and pencil for spinner

Instructions

1 Cut out the 24 cards on pages 3, 4 and 5.

2 Mix the cards and stack them face-down.

3 Using the game board on page 6, play the game.

- Each player draws a card.

- Players count by 5s and 1s to determine the worth of the cards.

- Compare the cards and place them where they belong on the game board. If the cards are equal, put them in the middle of the game board. The player who wins the next spin gets to take them.

- Spin the spinner to determine who gets to take the cards.

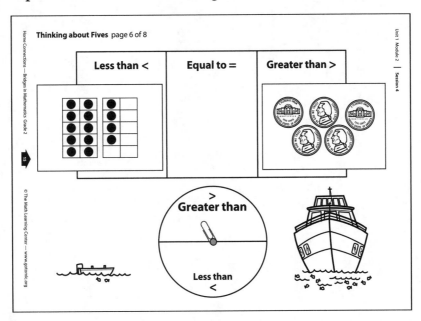

Child The spinner landed on greater than! I got 25 and you only got 14—I get to take both cards this time!

(continued on next page)

Thinking About Fives page 2 of 8

4 Continue playing until you are out of cards. The player with the most cards at the end wins.

5 Complete pages 7 and 8 and return them to your teacher.

(continued on next page)

8

Thinking About Fives page 3 of 8

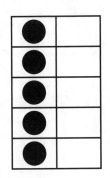

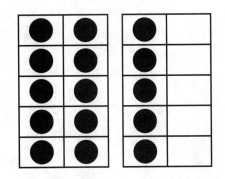

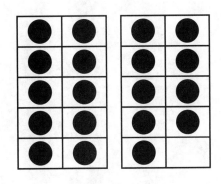

(continued on next page)

10

Thinking About Fives page 4 of 8

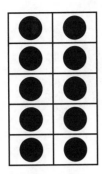

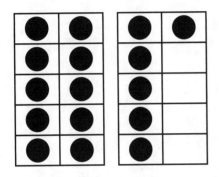

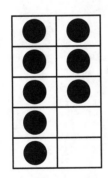

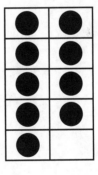

(continued on next page)

Thinking About Fives page 5 of 8

(continued on next page)

13

Thinking About Fives page 6 of 8

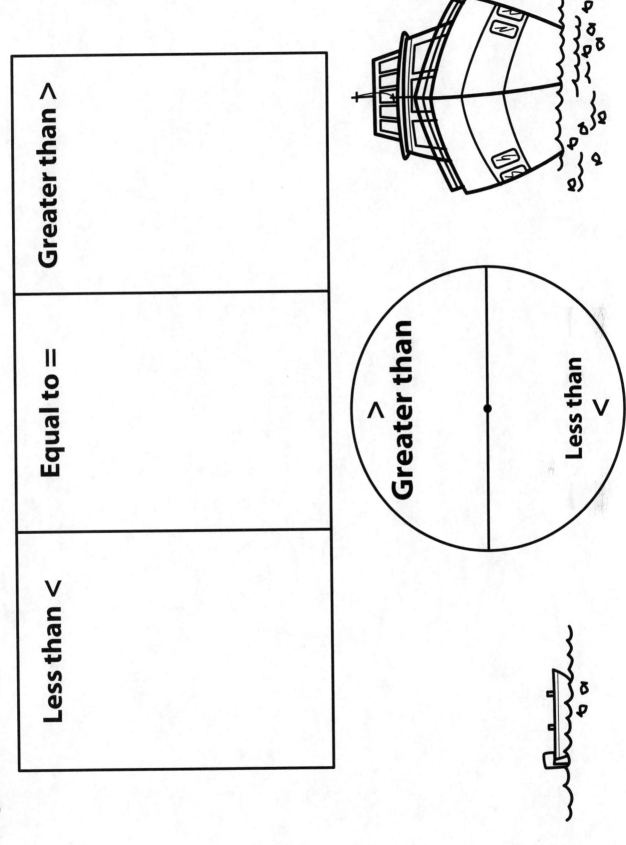

Less than <	Equal to =	Greater than >

15

NAME _____ | **DATE** _____

Thinking About Fives page 7 of 8

1 Write the 5s counting pattern to 50 under the ten-frames below. The first 3 numbers have been done for you.

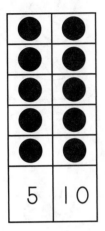 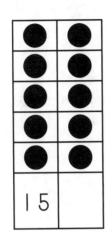 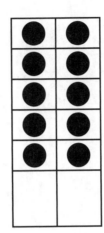 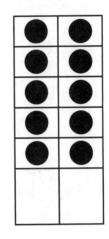

2 Solve these equations. Use the ten-frames above to help if you like.

$5 + 5 =$ _____ $15 + 5 =$ _____ $30 + 5 =$ _____ $25 + 5 =$ _____

$45 + 5 =$ _____ $5 - 5 =$ _____ $15 - 5 =$ _____ $30 - 5 =$ _____

$25 - 5 =$ _____ $45 - 5 =$ _____ $20 - 5 =$ _____ $35 + 5 =$ _____

(continued on next page)

NAME _____ | DATE _____

Thinking About Fives page 8 of 8

3 Answer the questions about fingers and toes.

3
hands

How many fingers in all? ___15___

8
feet

How many toes in all? ___45___

5
hands

How many fingers in all? ___25___

10
feet

How many toes in all? ___50___

4 **CHALLENGE** 35 toes—how many feet?

Hint Draw a picture to help.

_____ feet

🏠 Number Lines & Patterns page 1 of 2

1 Trace each number and then practice writing it twice.

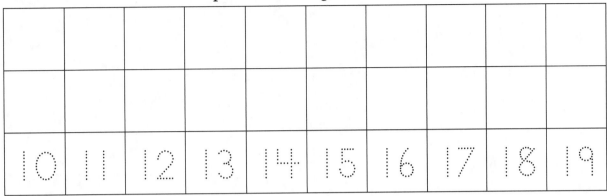

2 Fill in the missing numbers on each number line below.

a

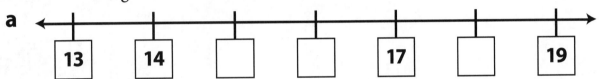

13 14 ☐ ☐ 17 ☐ 19

b

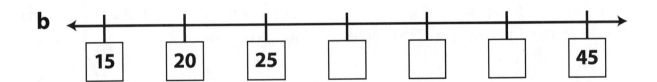

15 20 25 ☐ ☐ ☐ 45

c

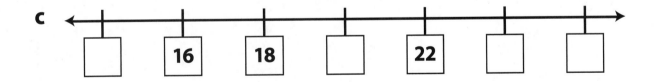

☐ 16 18 ☐ 22 ☐ ☐

d

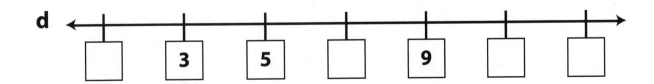

☐ 3 5 ☐ 9 ☐ ☐

(continued on next page)

NAME _____ | DATE _____

Number Lines & Patterns page 2 of 2

3 James had 13 baseball cards. He gave 6 to his brother. How many baseball cards does James have now? Show your work.

James has _____ baseball cards now.

4 **CHALLENGE** Mai threw 3 darts at the board. All 3 of them stuck in the board. What are all the different scores she could get? Show your work.

Searching for Pairs page 1 of 2

Note to Families

To practice the 2s counting pattern and just have a little fun, work with your child to find and list some of the many things around your house that come in pairs. Then have your child complete the rest of the assignment and return it to school.

1 Search your home for things that come in pairs, like shoes and mittens. What else can you find? List some of your discoveries below.

_____   _____

_____   _____

_____   _____

_____   _____

_____   _____

2 Think about a pair of mittens.

How many mittens are there in 1 pair? _____

How many mittens are there in 2 pairs? _____

How many mittens are there in 3 pairs? _____

3 Fill in the missing numbers on the Mittens Chart below.

Pairs of Mittens	1	2		4		6	7		9	10	20	30	100
Individual Mittens	2	4	6		10		16						

(continued on next page)

NAME _____ | DATE _____

Searching for Pairs page 2 of 2

4 Write the numbers from 1 to 30 in the grid below. Then color in just the even numbers, starting with 2.

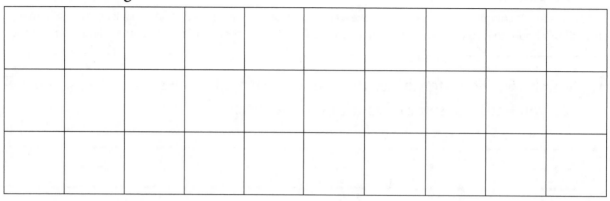

5 Solve these equations.

a   4 + 2 = _____   14 + 2 = _____   24 + 2 = _____   8 + 2 = _____

18 + 2 = _____   28 + 2 = _____   16 − 2 = _____   26 − 2 = _____

10 − 2 = _____   20 − 2 = _____   30 − 2 = _____   14 − 2 = _____

b   **CHALLENGE** Sam says the answers to all of these problems are even. Do you agree with Sam? Why or why not?

6 Answer the questions about these insects.

4
2-spotted
ladybugs

10
2-winged
flies

6
2-spotted
ladybugs

20
2-winged
flies

How many spots   How many wings   How many spots   How many wings

in all? _____   in all? _____   in all? _____   in all? _____

🏠 **Finding the Difference** page 1 of 2

1 Suzy Spider and Freddy Fly are playing another game of Battling Bugs. Fill in the sentence beside the strips to show the difference between their scores in each problem below. Write or complete a subtraction equation to match.

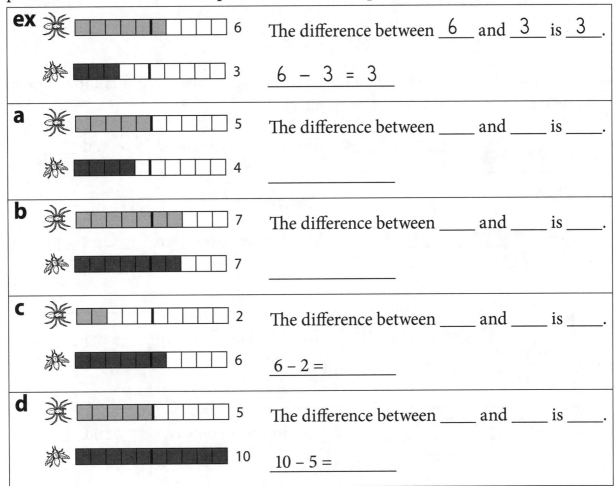

ex   6

The difference between __6__ and __3__ is __3__.

3

6 − 3 = 3

a   5

The difference between _____ and _____ is _____.

4

_____

b   7

The difference between _____ and _____ is _____.

7

_____

c   2

The difference between _____ and _____ is _____.

6

6 − 2 = _____

d   5

The difference between _____ and _____ is _____.

10

10 − 5 = _____

2 Add up each bug's points to find out who won the game.

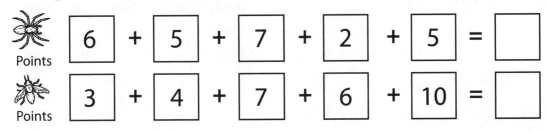

Points   6 + 5 + 7 + 2 + 5 = ☐

Points   3 + 4 + 7 + 6 + 10 = ☐

3 Which bug won? _____ By how many points? _____ Show your work.

(continued on next page)

NAME _____ | **DATE** _____

Finding the Difference page 2 of 2

You can use ten-strips to show the difference between two numbers. You can also use bars like this.

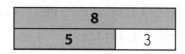

The difference between __8__ and __5__ is __3__.

$\underline{8 - 5 = 3}$

4 Label the white piece on each of the bar drawings below. Then fill in the sentence and write a subtraction equation to match.

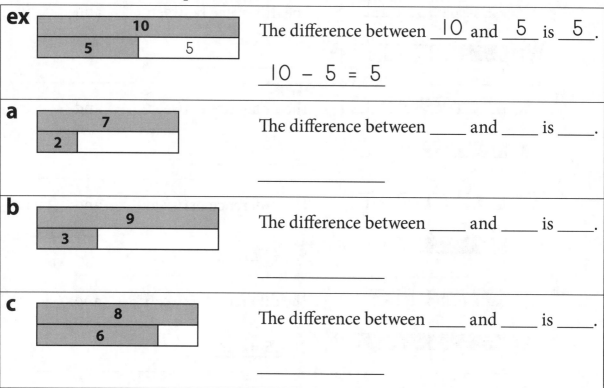

ex

The difference between __10__ and __5__ is __5__.

$\underline{10 - 5 = 5}$

a

The difference between ____ and ____ is ____.

_____

b

The difference between ____ and ____ is ____.

_____

c

The difference between ____ and ____ is ____.

_____

5 CHALLENGE Gretchen and her dad went to the football game last week. By the end of the second quarter, the Vikings had 6 points and the Ducks had 21 points. The Vikings scored 23 more points before the end of the game, and the Ducks scored 13 more points.

a Which team won the game?

b How many points did they win by? Use sketches, numbers, and/or words to explain your answer.

NAME _____ | **DATE** _____

More Story Problems page 1 of 2

A story problem gives you some facts and asks a question. For each problem:

- Underline the facts.
- Put a box around the question.
- Solve the problem and show your work.
- Write the answer on the line.

ex <u>There were 7 ladybugs on the leaf. Then 6 more landed on the leaf.</u> | How many ladybugs in all? |

$$7 + 6 = 13$$

There were __13__ ladybugs in all.

1 There were 10 ladybugs sitting on a leaf. A bird came and chased 4 of them away. How many ladybugs were left?

_____ ladybugs were left.

2 There are 4 ladybugs on the leaf. How many legs in all? (Ladybugs have 6 legs.)

There are _____ legs in all.

(continued on next page)

More Story Problems page 2 of 2

3 There were 5 ladybugs on a leaf. Some more ladybugs came. Then there were 12 ladybugs on the leaf. How many ladybugs came?

_____ ladybugs came.

4 Mark has 3 dogs, 5 cats, and 8 fish. How many pets does he have in all? Show your work.

Mark has _____ pets in all.

5 **CHALLENGE** Here are two clues.

- Carly has 2 more nickels than dimes in her pocket.
- She has 40 cents.

How many nickels does Carly have? How many dimes does Carly have? Show your work.

Carly has _____ nickels. Carly has _____ dimes.

NAME _____ **| DATE** _____

 Fact Strategy Practice page 1 of 2

1 Color the ten-strips to match each addition problem. Write the answer.

ex
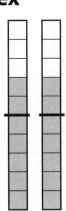
$\begin{array}{r} 7 \\ + 7 \\ \hline 14 \end{array}$

a
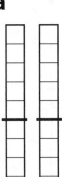
$\begin{array}{r} 7 \\ + 8 \\ \hline \end{array}$

b
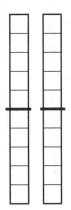
$\begin{array}{r} 6 \\ + 6 \\ \hline \end{array}$

c
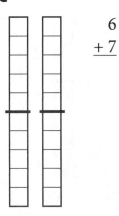
$\begin{array}{r} 6 \\ + 7 \\ \hline \end{array}$

d
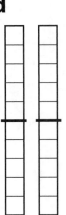
$\begin{array}{r} 8 \\ + 8 \\ \hline \end{array}$

e
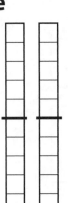
$\begin{array}{r} 9 \\ + 8 \\ \hline \end{array}$

f
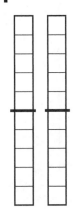
$\begin{array}{r} 9 \\ + 9 \\ \hline \end{array}$

g
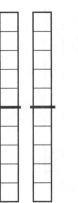
$\begin{array}{r} 10 \\ + 9 \\ \hline \end{array}$

2 Find each difference.

| $\begin{array}{r}10\\-5\\\hline\end{array}$ | $\begin{array}{r}11\\-5\\\hline\end{array}$ | $\begin{array}{r}8\\-4\\\hline\end{array}$ | $\begin{array}{r}9\\-4\\\hline\end{array}$ | $\begin{array}{r}6\\-3\\\hline\end{array}$ | $\begin{array}{r}7\\-3\\\hline\end{array}$ | $\begin{array}{r}4\\-2\\\hline\end{array}$ |

| $\begin{array}{r}14\\-7\\\hline\end{array}$ | $\begin{array}{r}15\\-7\\\hline\end{array}$ | $\begin{array}{r}12\\-6\\\hline\end{array}$ | $\begin{array}{r}13\\-6\\\hline\end{array}$ | $\begin{array}{r}16\\-8\\\hline\end{array}$ | $\begin{array}{r}17\\-8\\\hline\end{array}$ | $\begin{array}{r}18\\-9\\\hline\end{array}$ |

(continued on next page)

NAME | DATE

Fact Strategy Practice page 2 of 2

3 Color the ten-strips to match each addition problem. Write the answer.

ex

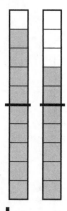

$\begin{array}{r} 9 \\ + 7 \\ \hline 16 \end{array}$

a

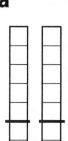

$\begin{array}{r} 9 \\ + 3 \\ \hline \end{array}$

b

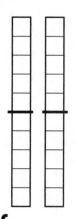

$\begin{array}{r} 6 \\ + 9 \\ \hline \end{array}$

c

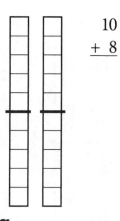

$\begin{array}{r} 10 \\ + 8 \\ \hline \end{array}$

d

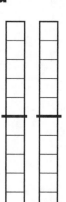

$\begin{array}{r} 9 \\ + 5 \\ \hline \end{array}$

e

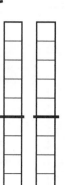

$\begin{array}{r} 4 \\ + 9 \\ \hline \end{array}$

f

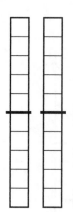

$\begin{array}{r} 9 \\ + 8 \\ \hline \end{array}$

g

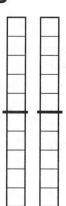

$\begin{array}{r} 10 \\ + 7 \\ \hline \end{array}$

4 Find each difference.

$\begin{array}{r} 16 \\ -10 \\ \hline \end{array}$	$\begin{array}{r} 16 \\ -9 \\ \hline \end{array}$	$\begin{array}{r} 12 \\ -10 \\ \hline \end{array}$	$\begin{array}{r} 12 \\ -9 \\ \hline \end{array}$	$\begin{array}{r} 15 \\ -10 \\ \hline \end{array}$	$\begin{array}{r} 15 \\ -9 \\ \hline \end{array}$	$\begin{array}{r} 18 \\ -10 \\ \hline \end{array}$

$\begin{array}{r} 18 \\ -9 \\ \hline \end{array}$	$\begin{array}{r} 14 \\ -10 \\ \hline \end{array}$	$\begin{array}{r} 14 \\ -9 \\ \hline \end{array}$	$\begin{array}{r} 13 \\ -10 \\ \hline \end{array}$	$\begin{array}{r} 13 \\ -9 \\ \hline \end{array}$	$\begin{array}{r} 17 \\ -10 \\ \hline \end{array}$	$\begin{array}{r} 17 \\ -9 \\ \hline \end{array}$

NAME _____ | **DATE** _____

 These Beans Have Got To Go! page 1 of 4

Note to Families

Winning is not just a matter of luck in this game where players take turns spinning and adding. Certain sums are going to come up more often than others. It is easier to spin a total of 7 than a total of 2, for instance, simply because there are more combinations for 7 on the spinners. You can get a 7 by spinning 1 + 6 or 2 + 5 or 3 + 4. The only way to get a 2 is by spinning 1 + 1. Your child will probably want to place a bean on every number "just to be safe," but will learn through experience that the middle numbers usually come up more often. The second part of the assignment will help them find out why.

Materials

- These Beans Have Got To Go! pages 1–4
- 24 game pieces, 12 each in 2 different colors (e.g., 12 lima and 12 pinto beans, 12 red and 12 white buttons, 12 pennies and 12 dimes, 12 red and 12 yellow Legos)
- paperclip and pencil for spinner
- crayons or colored pencils

Instructions

1 Each player should place his or her beans on the game board (page 2).

Note You can place more than 1 bean on a particular number.

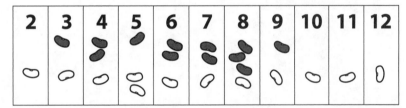

2 Players take turns spinning two numbers, adding them, and removing a game piece.

- The first player spins both spinners and adds the two numbers.
- If the player has any beans on that total, she can remove one bean from that section of the board. Her turn is over.
- If there are no beans on that total, the player's turn is over.

3 Continue playing until one player moves all the beans from his or her board. This player is the winner.

4 Play the game several times and talk about ideas that would help someone win. (Hint: You might want to do pages 3 and 4 of this assignment first.)

(continued on next page)

These Beans Have Got To Go! page 2 of 4

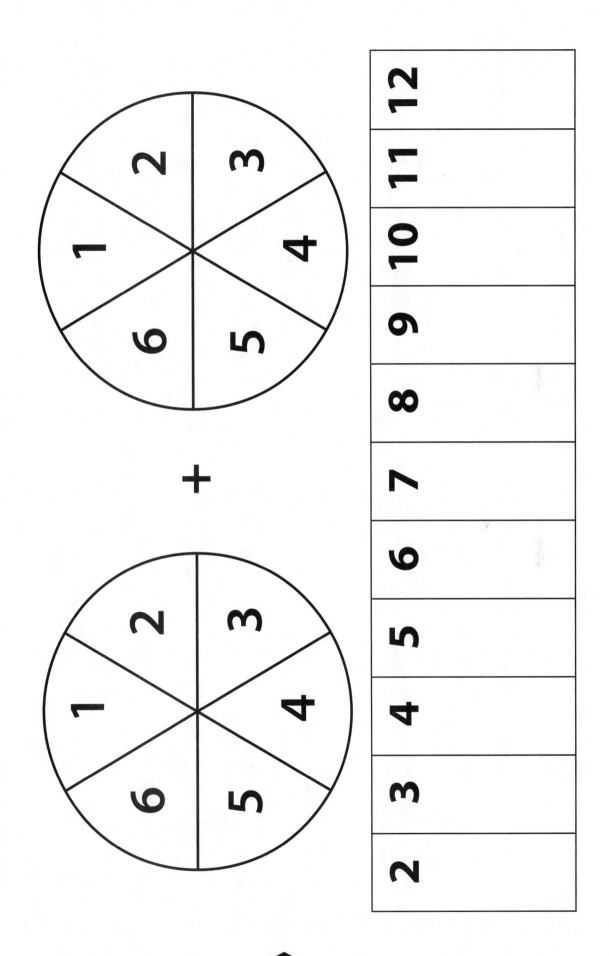

31

These Beans Have Got To Go! page 3 of 4

Are you wondering why the middle numbers keep winning on the the game you just played? Fill in the sums on the addition table shown below and follow the instructions for coloring them in—you might begin to see why it's a better idea to put your beans on the 6 and the 7 instead of the 2 and the 12.

1 Fill in the sums on the addition table below.

2 Color in the table using the rules below.
- 6s red
- 7s orange
- 8s yellow

+	1	2	3	4	5	6
1	2	3				
2						
3			6			
4						
5		7				
6						

(continued on next page)

33

These Beans Have Got To Go! page 4 of 4

3 Which sums came up the most often on the addition table?

4 Which came up the least often on the addition table?

5 Why do you think it worked this way?

Tens, Dollars & Quarters page 1 of 2

1 Circle the two numbers in each box that add up to 10.

ex	a	b	c
⑨ 3	5 4	7 2	2 8
5 ①	6 2	3 0	5 3

2 Write two addition equations and two subtraction equations to match each ten-frame.

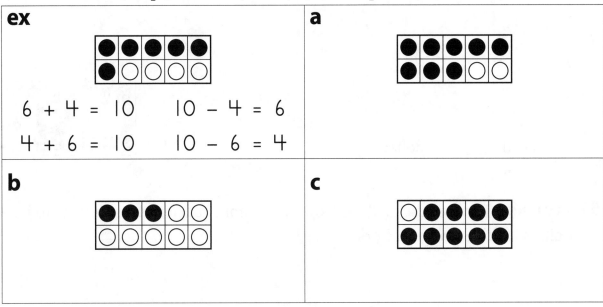

ex

6 + 4 = 10   10 − 4 = 6

4 + 6 = 10   10 − 6 = 4

a

b

c

3 Find each difference.

10	10	10	10	10	10	10
− 7	− 5	− 6	− 3	− 4	− 9	− 2

4 Fill in the missing numbers.

3 + _____ = 10   _____ + 5 = 10   4 + 6 = _____   9 + _____ = 10

10 = 7 + _____   10 = 8 + _____   6 + _____ = 10   1 + 4 + 5 = _____

(continued on next page)

NAME _____ | DATE _____

Tens, Dollars & Quarters page 2 of 2

5 Jana has 7 dollars. How many more dollars does she need to have 14 dollars in all? Show your work.

Jana needs _____ dollars.

6 **CHALLENGE** Timmy has 7 dollars. How many more quarters does he need to have 12 dollars in all? Show your work.

Timmy needs _____ more quarters.

36

🏠 Cubes & Tens page 1 of 2

1 Write a number to show how many tens and ones are in each box below.

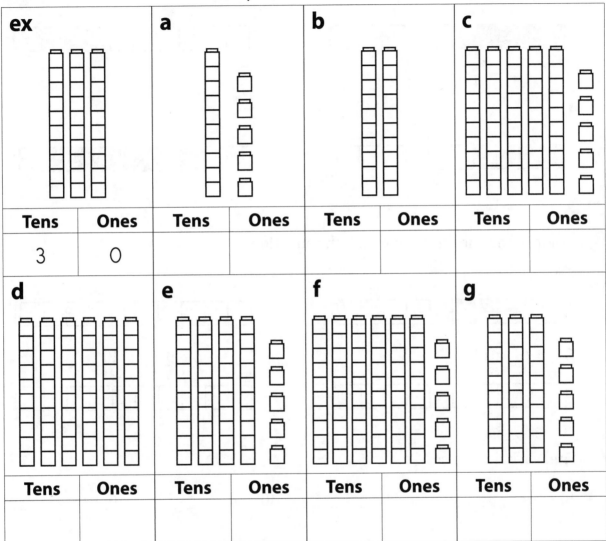

ex		a		b		c	
Tens	Ones	Tens	Ones	Tens	Ones	Tens	Ones
3	0						

d		e		f		g	
Tens	Ones	Tens	Ones	Tens	Ones	Tens	Ones

2 Fill in the missing numbers on the number line below.

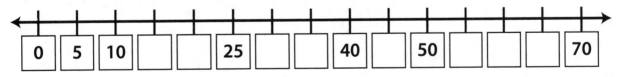

| 0 | 5 | 10 | | | 25 | | | 40 | | 50 | | | | 70 |

3 Find each sum.

20	10	30	40	50	15	25
+ 10	+ 5	+ 8	+ 6	+ 10	+ 5	+ 5

(continued on next page)

NAME _____ | DATE _____

Cubes & Tens page 2 of 2

4 Write an equation to match each cube train.

ex

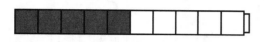

5 + 5 = 10

a

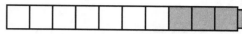

b

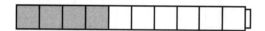

c

5 Color in the cube train to match the equation.

ex 6 + 4 = 10

a 8 + 2 = 10

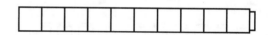

b 3 + 7 = 10

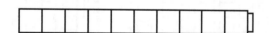

c 1 + 2 + 3 + 4 = 10

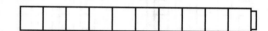

6 Find each difference.

10 – 0 = _____   10 – 3 = _____   10 – 9 = _____   10 – 2 = _____

10 – 4 = _____   10 – 1 = _____   10 – 5 = _____   10 – 8 = _____

9 – 4 = _____   10 – 6 = _____   10 – 7 = _____   10 – 10 = _____

7 Fill in the missing numbers.

5 + _____ = 10   _____ + 7 = 10   10 = 6 + _____   10 = 1 + _____

NAME _____ **DATE** _____

 # Add, Subtract & Compare page 1 of 2

1 Fill in the missing numbers on the addition tables. Some of the numbers have already been filled in for you.

a

+	2	3	4	5	6	7
1	3					
2			6			
3						10
4						
5		8			11	
6						

b

+	3	4	5	6	7	8
3	6					
4			9			
5						13
6						
7		11			14	
8						

2 Fill in the missing numbers on the subtraction tables. Some of the numbers have already been filled in for you.

a

0	1	2	3	4	5	–
		2				0
				3		1
						2
			0			3
						4
						5

b

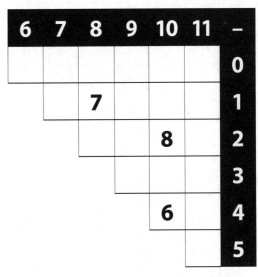

6	7	8	9	10	11	–
						0
	7					1
			8			2
						3
				6		4
						5

(continued on next page)

NAME _____ | DATE _____

Add, Subtract & Compare page 2 of 2

3 Here are six pairs of Unifix cube collections. For each pair, write a mathematical statement to show exactly how many cubes are in each collection, as well as which is greater and which is less.

< less than   = equal to   > greater than

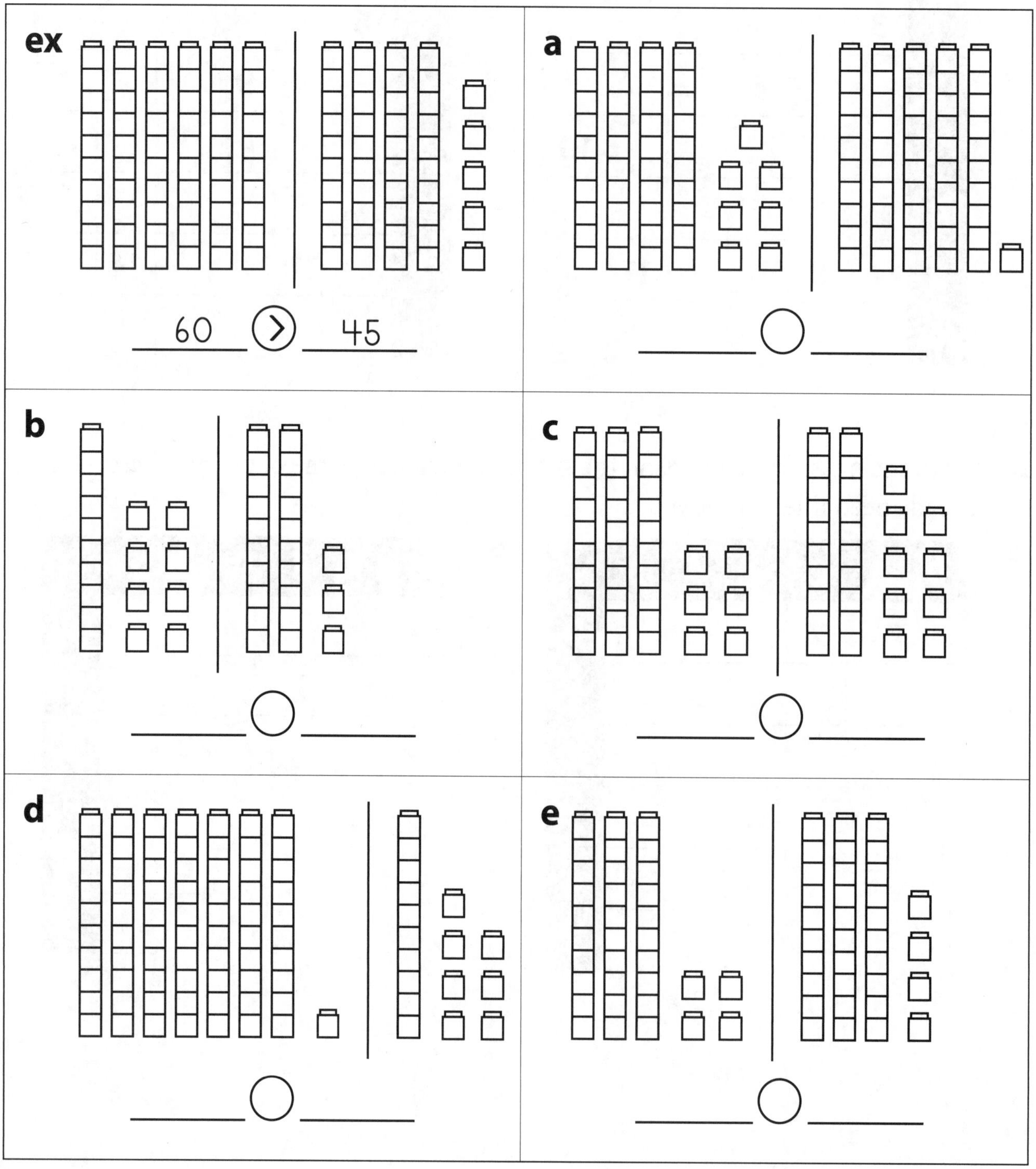

ex

_60_ (>) _45_

a

_____ ◯ _____

b

_____ ◯ _____

c

_____ ◯ _____

d

_____ ◯ _____

e

_____ ◯ _____

NAME _____ | DATE _____

 # Place Value Showdown page 1 of 6

Note to Families

This game uses drawings to stand for numbers. The little square unit stands for 1, the strip of ten stands for 10, and the mat of one hundred stands for 100. If you have a collection of 2 mats, 3 strips, and 4 units, you're looking at 234. Place Value Showdown will help your child become more comfortable reading, understanding, and comparing 2- and 3-digit numbers. After you have played the game once or twice, have your child use the game cards to complete the written assignment on the last page. Return the written portion to school, but keep the game at home to play again.

Materials

- Place Value Showdown, pages 1–6
- Place Value Showdown cards, cut out from pages 2–5

Instructions

1 Cut out the cards on the 3 attached sheets. Mix them thoroughly and place them in a stack, face-down.

2 Take turns drawing a card and reporting how many units you see. The person with the card that's worth more gets to take both.

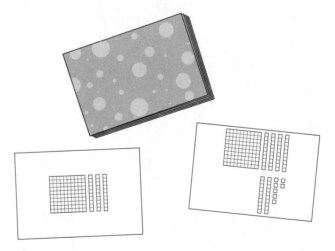

Child *I got 167. What did you get, Dad?*
Adult *I only got 130. You get this pair!*

3 Continue until there are no cards left. The player with the most cards wins.

4 Shuffle the cards and play again.

42

Place Value Showdown page 2 of 6

44

Place Value Showdown page 3 of 6

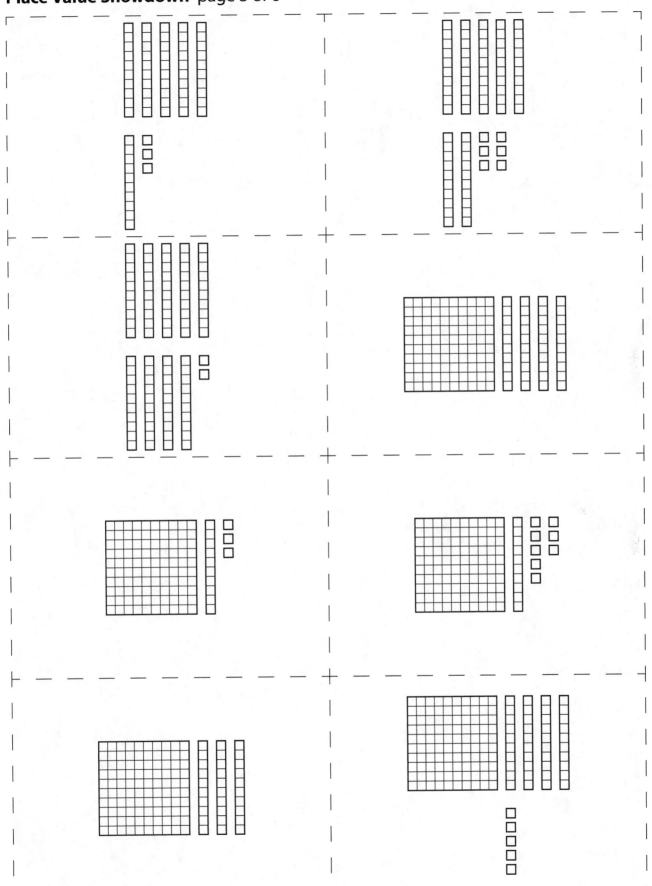

45

Place Value Showdown page 4 of 6

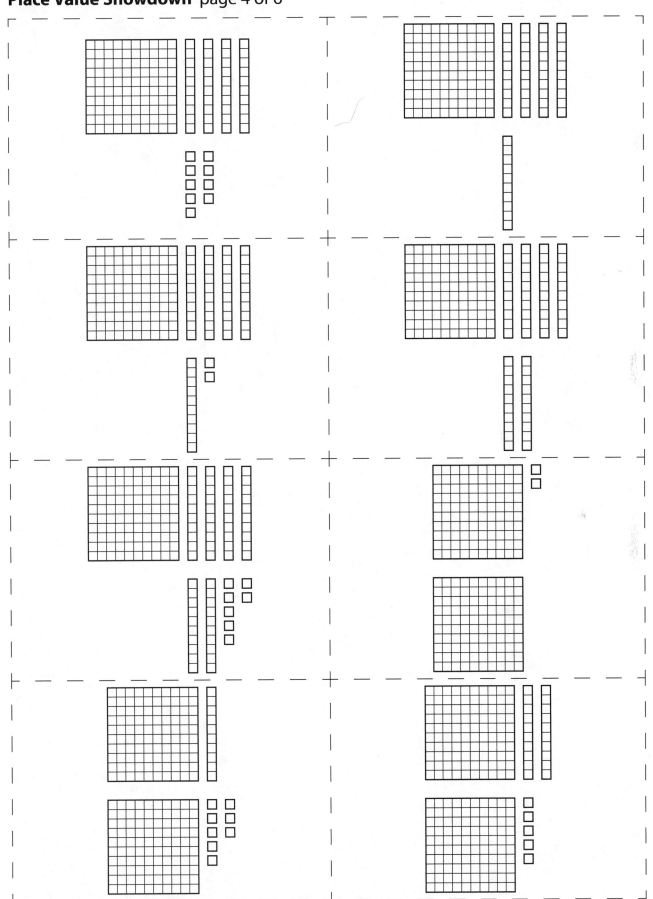

47

Place Value Showdown page 5 of 6

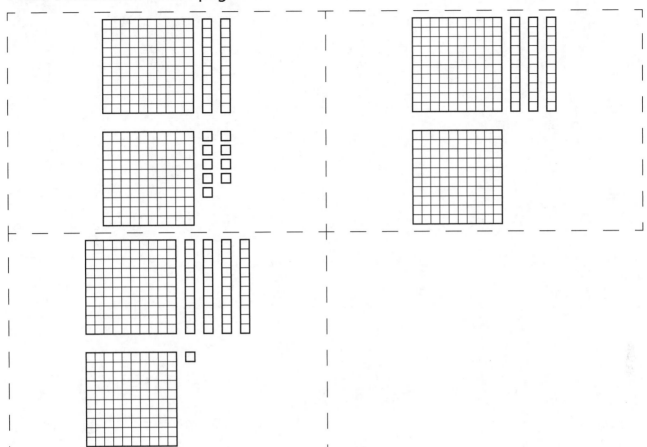

49

NAME _____ | **DATE** _____

Place Value Showdown page 6 of 6

1 Take all the game cards you just used to play Place Value Showdown and put them in order from the lowest to the highest. Then record the numbers in order on the lines below. The first three have been done for you.

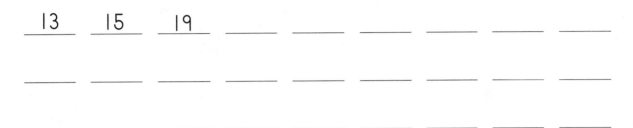

_13_ _15_ _19_ ___ ___ ___ ___ ___ ___

___ ___ ___ ___ ___ ___ ___ ___ ___

___ ___ ___ ___ ___ ___ ___ ___ ___

2 Add.

$$\begin{array}{r} 26 \\ + 10 \\ \hline \end{array}$$

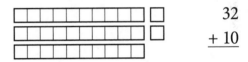
$$\begin{array}{r} 32 \\ + 10 \\ \hline \end{array}$$

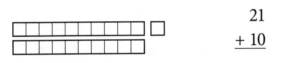
$$\begin{array}{r} 21 \\ + 10 \\ \hline \end{array}$$

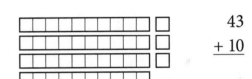
$$\begin{array}{r} 43 \\ + 10 \\ \hline \end{array}$$

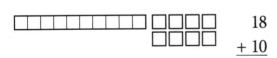
$$\begin{array}{r} 18 \\ + 10 \\ \hline \end{array}$$

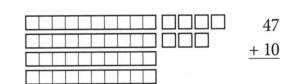
$$\begin{array}{r} 47 \\ + 10 \\ \hline \end{array}$$

3 What happens every time you add 10 to a number?

🏠 Addition & Subtraction Practice page 1 of 2

1 Complete the problems below.

a Circle all the +2 facts in blue. Then find each sum.

b Circle all the +10 facts in red. Then find each sum.

2	10	2	5	7	9	2
+ 6	+ 1	+ 8	+ 2	+ 2	+ 10	+ 4

10	10	2	2	10	6	11
+ 4	+ 7	+ 8	+ 2	+ 3	+ 10	+ 2

2 Complete the problems below.

a Circle all the –2 facts in blue. Then find each difference.

b Circle all the –10 facts in red. Then find each difference.

10	14	6	9	12	19	7
– 2	– 10	– 2	– 2	– 10	– 10	– 2

13	17	4	16	14	18	11
– 2	– 10	– 2	– 10	– 2	– 10	– 2

15	20	5	8	11	20	3
– 2	– 10	– 2	– 2	– 10	– 10	– 2

3 True or false? Circle one.

a $10 + 5 = 15$ T   F   **b** $7 + 7 = 13$ T   F   **c** $5 + 6 = 11$ T   F

d $13 - 3 = 8$ T   F   **e** $14 - 7 = 7$ T   F   **f** $19 - 10 = 9$ T   F

(continued on next page)

53

NAME _____ | DATE _____

Addition & Subtraction Practice page 2 of 2

Sometimes story problems give you more facts than you need to solve the problem. In each problem below, cross out the information you don't need. Then solve the problem. Show your work.

4 Neena bought 7 red apples, 8 green apples, and 3 yellow apples. Neena is 12 years old. How many apples did Neena buy?

Neena bought _____ apples.

5 Pedro had 15 dollars. He spent 9 dollars on a book. His friend had 12 dollars. How much money did Pedro have left?

Pedro had _____ dollars left.

6 The gym teacher had 16 soccer balls. She had 14 footballs. She gave 8 of the soccer balls to the playground helper. How many soccer balls did she have left?

The gym teacher had _____ soccer balls left.

7 CHALLENGE The ladybug ate 28 aphids in the morning. Then she took a nap on a leaf for 3 hours. She ate 34 aphids in the afternoon. How many aphids did she eat in all?

The ladybug ate _____ aphids in all.

NAME _____ | DATE _____

 Tens & Time page 1 of 2

1 Make Ten facts are pairs of numbers that add up to 10, like 5 + 5, 4 + 6, and 8 + 2.

a Circle all the Make Ten facts in red. Then find each sum.

b Circle all the facts that are *not* Make Ten facts in blue. Then find each sum.

4	6	3	5	4	9	4
+ 6	+ 1	+ 8	+ 5	+ 3	+ 1	+ 4

5	3	2	7	6	5	10
+ 4	+ 7	+ 8	+ 2	+ 3	+ 3	+ 0

6	6	5	3	1	2	3
+ 1	+ 4	+ 5	+ 7	+ 9	+ 2	+ 6

2 Find each sum. Use the Make Ten facts to help.

ex 4 + ⑤ + 2 + ⑤ = __16__
        ___10___/

ex ⑧ + ③ + ② + ⑦ = __20__
        10   10

a 2 + 9 + 1 + 6 = _____

b 3 + 4 + 8 + 2 = _____

c 3 + 7 + 4 + 6 = _____

d 3 + 3 + 5 + 5 = _____

e 6 + 5 + 5 + 9 + 1 = _____

f 7 + 2 + 3 + 7 + 1 = _____

(continued on next page)

55

NAME | **DATE**

Tens & Time page 2 of 2

Time Problems

We use the abbreviations a.m. and p.m. (or with capital letters as A.M. and P.M.).

People often say that times in the a.m. are morning times, but a.m. really indicates any time between midnight and noon.

People often say that times in the p.m. are times in the afternoon or night. But p.m. really indicates any time between noon and midnight.

When it's 3:00 a.m., it is so early in the morning that it's not even light yet. Most people are asleep. When it's 3:00 p.m. in the afternoon, that's just about the time school gets out. Most people are awake at 3:00 p.m.

3 Circle the time that people would probably do each of these things on a school day.

	Activity		a.m.	p.m.
a	Eat dinner		6:00 a.m.	6:00 p.m.
b	Eat breakfast		7:00 a.m.	7:00 p.m.
c	Watch TV		5:00 a.m.	5:00 p.m.
d	Do homework		4:00 a.m.	4:00 p.m.
e	Turn on a night-light		8:30 a.m.	8:30 p.m.
f	Ride a bike		3:30 a.m.	3:30 p.m.

4 On another piece of paper, draw a picture of something you do at 10:00 a.m. on a school day.

Facts & Numbers page 1 of 2

1 Complete the problems below.

a Circle all the Doubles facts (e.g., 10 + 10) in blue. Then find each sum.

b Circle all the Doubles Plus or Minus One facts (e.g., 4 + 5) in red.
Then find each sum.

2	2	5	5	4	4	6
+ 2	+ 3	+ 5	+ 6	+ 3	+ 4	+ 6

6	6	7	8	9	9	11
+ 5	+ 7	+ 7	+ 7	+ 9	+ 10	+ 11

3	3	8	12	12	13	13
+ 3	+ 4	+ 8	+ 12	+ 13	+ 13	+ 14

2 Complete the problems below.

a Circle all the Half facts (e.g., 8 – 4) in blue. Then find each difference.

b Circle all the Take Away Ten facts in red. Then find each difference.

10	15	6	19	13	14	4
– 5	– 10	– 3	– 10	– 10	– 7	– 2

16	20	12	40	60	100	80
– 8	– 10	– 6	– 20	– 30	– 50	– 40

3 True or false? Circle one.

a 6 + 7 = 13   T   F   **b** 9 + 8 = 17   T   F   **c** 5 + 5 = 9   T   F

d 14 – 7 = 8   T   F   **e** 16 – 8 = 10   T   F   **f** 12 – 6 = 6   T   F

(continued on next page)

NAME | **DATE**

Facts & Numbers page 2 of 2

4 Trace the numerals and the words.

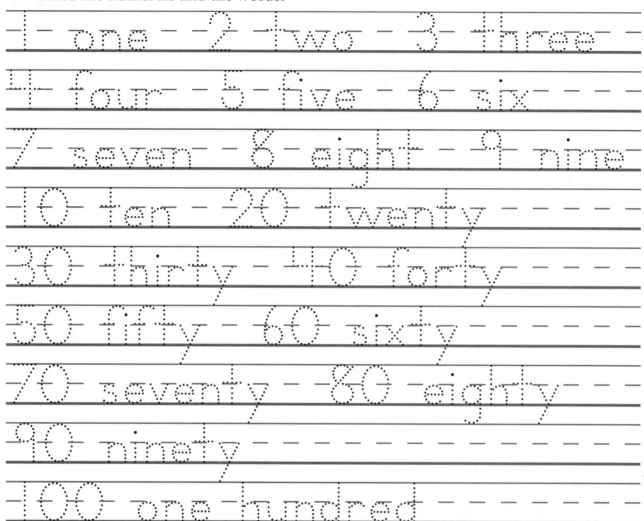

1 one — 2 two — 3 three —
4 four — 5 five — 6 six — —
7 seven — 8 eight — 9 nine —
10 ten — 20 twenty — — —
30 thirty — 40 forty
50 fifty — 60 sixty
70 seventy — 80 eighty
90 ninety — — — —
100 one hundred — — — —

5 Write words to label each set of base ten pieces with the correct number.

ex ninety-four

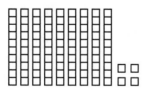

a _____

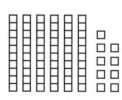

b _____

c _____

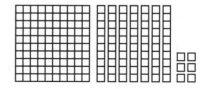

Make Tens page 1 of 2

1 Make Ten facts are pairs of numbers that add up to 10, like 9 + 1, 4 + 6, and 3 + 7.

a Circle all the Make Ten facts in red. Then find each sum.

b Circle all the facts that are *not* Make Ten facts in blue. Then find each sum.

7	6	2	7	5	10	5
+ 3	+ 6	+ 8	+ 7	+ 5	+ 0	+ 4

6	3	8	7	6	9	0
+ 7	+ 7	+ 8	+ 8	+ 4	+ 9	+ 10

10	1	4	3	4	2	10
+ 10	+ 9	+ 6	+ 2	+ 3	+ 8	+ 9

2 Find each sum. Use the Make Ten facts to help.

ex 3 + ⑥ + 6 + ④ = __19__

ex ⑧ + ⑤ + ② + ⑤ + 4 = __24__

a 3 + 7 + 9 + 1 = _____

b 2 + 6 + 4 + 2 = _____

c 9 + 5 + 5 + 3 + 7 = _____

d 8 + 2 + 5 + 2 + 5 = _____

3 Find each difference.

10 − 6 = _____   10 − 8 = _____   10 − 5 = _____   10 − 3 = _____

10 − 9 = _____   10 − 1 = _____   10 − 4 = _____   10 − 2 = _____

(continued on next page)

NAME | **DATE**

Make Tens page 2 of 2

Number Line Problems

DJ Hopper says you can use what you know about Making Tens to help subtract.

If the fact is 15 – 9, you can think about making a ten (9 + 1 = 10) and then adding 5 more to get to 15. DJ likes to show his work on the number line, like this.

15 – 9 = 6

1 Make hops on the number line and label them to solve subtraction problems.

ex 14 – 8 = _____6_____

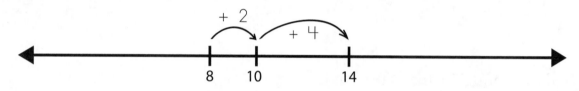

a 13 – 7 = _____

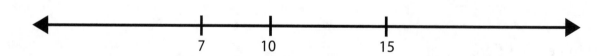

b 15 – 7 = _____

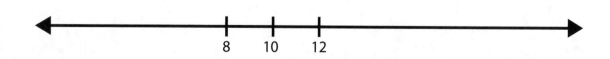

c 12 – 8 = _____

60

NAME | **DATE**

 Twos & More page 1 of 2

1 Fill in the missing numbers. Then color in the count-by-2s numbers, starting with 2 (2, 4, 6, 8, and so on).

1			4					9	
	12			15					20
			24			27			
	33				36		38		

2 Find each sum.

6 + 2 = _____   2 + 10 = _____   24 + 2 = _____   2 + 12 = _____

18 + 2 = _____   30 + 2 = _____   14 + 2 = _____   8 + 2 = _____

3 Find each difference.

8 – 2 = _____   12 – 2 = _____   16 – 2 = _____   10 – 2 = _____

28 – 2 = _____   36 – 2 = _____   24 – 2 = _____   40 – 2 = _____

4 Fill in the blanks.

9
leaf-cutter ants

12
birds

7
elephants

How many antennae

in all? _____

How many wings

in all? _____

How many ears

in all? _____

(continued on next page)

61

NAME | **DATE**

Twos & More page 2 of 2

5 Rosa had 13 fish in the tank. She put some in her brother's fish bowl. Now Rosa has only 9 fish in the tank. How many did she give to her brother?

She gave her brother _____ fish.

6 **CHALLENGE** Find different ways to make 23¢. Finish the chart. Be sure to fill in every box.

	Dimes	Nickels	Pennies
ex	2	0	3
ex	1	2	3
a	1	1	
b	1	0	
c	0	4	
d	0		
e	0		
f	0		
g	0		

Steps & Leaps page 1 of 6

Note to Families

This Home Connection is a game that students have been playing at school. In Steps & Leaps, players work on separate sheets to try to be first to reach or cross the 100th space. They take turns rolling two dice to determine the number of small steps to take forward and spinning a spinner to leap forward by 10s. As you play, encourage your student to find ways to count by 5s or 10s to move forward on the board.

Materials

- Steps & Leaps pages 1–6
- pencil and paperclip to make a spinner
- 2 dice numbered or dotted 1-6
- 2 small objects (beans, buttons, etc.) for game markers

Instructions

1   Give each player a game board (one of pages 3–6) and a game marker. Write your name on your game board and roll the dice to choose which player will go first.

2   Have the first player roll the dice and spin the spinner to move around his or her game board.

- Roll the dice. Move forward that many spaces, and record the number of the square on the space where you land.

- Spin the spinner on the next page using a pencil and paperclip. Leap forward by that many 10s. Record the numbers of the squares where you land each time you take a leap of 10.

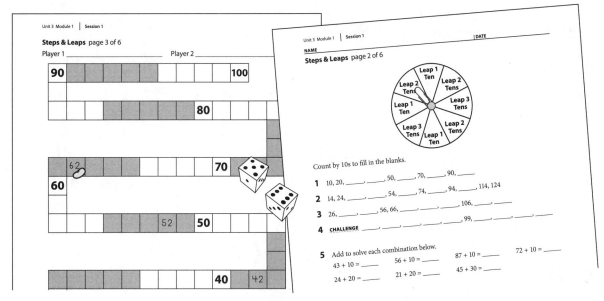

I was on 31. I rolled 11 and stepped to 42. I spun 2 tens, so I took 2 jumps by 10s and landed on 52 and 62.

3   After the steps and leaps are recorded, the other player rolls, spins, and records their steps and leaps on their own game board. The first player to reach or cross over 100 is the winner.

4   Using the other two game boards, play the game again. Then complete the problems on page 2 and return this sheet to school.

(continued on next page)

NAME _____ | DATE _____

Steps & Leaps page 2 of 6

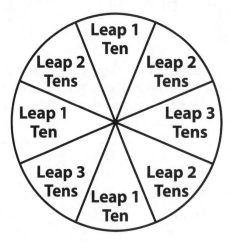

Count by 10s to fill in the blanks.

1 10, 20, _____, _____, 50, _____, 70, _____, 90, _____

2 14, 24, _____, _____, 54, _____, 74, _____, 94, _____, 114, 124

3 26, _____, _____, 56, 66, _____, _____, _____, 106, _____, _____

4 CHALLENGE _____, _____, _____, _____, _____, 99, _____, _____, _____, _____

5 Add to solve each combination below.

43 + 10 = _____   56 + 10 = _____   87 + 10 = _____   72 + 10 = _____

24 + 20 = _____   21 + 20 = _____   45 + 30 = _____

6 Subtract to solve each combination below.

15 − 10 = _____   19 − 10 = _____   23 − 10 = _____   34 − 20 = _____

56 − 20 = _____   88 − 30 = _____   97 + 40 = _____

7 CHALLENGE Solve the equations below.

120 + 50 + 20 − 40 = _____   330 − 20 + 50 − 60 = _____

500 − 50 − 40 − 20 + 120 = _____

(continued on next page)

Steps & Leaps page 3 of 6

Player 1 _____   Player 2 _____

| 90 | | | | | | | | | | 100 |

| 80 |

| 70 |

| 60 |

| 50 |

| 40 |

| 30 |

| 20 |

| 1 | | | | | | | | | 10 |

Steps & Leaps page 4 of 6

Player 1 _____   Player 2 _____

| 90 | | | | | | | | | | 100 |

| 80 |

| 60 |

| 70 |

| 50 |

| 40 |

| 30 |

| 20 |

| 1 | | | | | | | | | 10 |

Steps & Leaps page 5 of 6

Player 1 _____ Player 2 _____

| 90 | | | | | | | | | 100 |

| 80 |

| 70 |

| 60 |

| 50 |

| 40 |

| 30 |

| 20 |

| 1 | | | | | | | | | 10 |

Steps & Leaps page 6 of 6

Player 1 _____   Player 2 _____

| 90 | | | | | | | | | 100 |

| 80 |

| 60 |

| 70 |

| 50 |

| 30 |

| 40 |

| 20 |

| 1 | | | | | | | | 10 |

NAME _____ **DATE** _____

🏠 Puzzles & Shapes page 1 of 2

1 Fill in the missing numbers to solve these equations. Use the pictures to help.

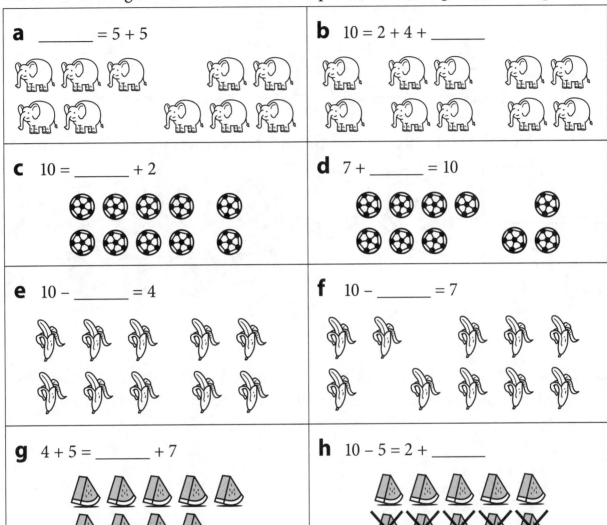

a _____ = 5 + 5

b 10 = 2 + 4 + _____

c 10 = _____ + 2

d 7 + _____ = 10

e 10 – _____ = 4

f 10 – _____ = 7

g 4 + 5 = _____ + 7

h 10 – 5 = 2 + _____

2 Fill in the missing numbers to solve these equations.

5 + 4 + 1 = _____   6 + 4 + _____ = 13   5 + _____ + 9 = 19

16 – _____ = 6   14 – _____ = 7   12 – 6 = _____

10 – 3 = 2 + _____   12 – 6 = 2 + _____   16 – 8 = _____ + 1

3 **CHALLENGE** Fill in the missing numbers to solve these equations.

90 – 30 = 20 + _____   143 – 11 = 127 + _____   160 – 18 = _____ + 15

(continued on next page)

NAME _____ | DATE _____

Puzzles & Shapes page 2 of 2

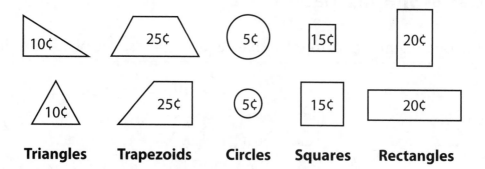

Triangles   Trapezoids   Circles   Squares   Rectangles

4 How much does this shape picture cost? Circle the coins you could use to pay for it.

5 Draw a vehicle (car, boat, truck, plane, scooter, bike, skateboard) that costs 75¢. Label your picture with the prices. Add the numbers to check your work.

NAME | **DATE**

🏠 Subtracting on the Line & Solving Story Problems page 1 of 2

DJ Hopper says you can use what you know about making 10 to help subtract.

If the fact is 15 – 8, you can think about making 10 (8 + 2 = 10) and then adding 5 more to get to 15. DJ likes to show his work on the number line, like this.

ex 15 – 8 = ___7___

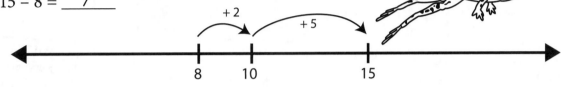

1 Make hops on the number line and label them to solve subtraction problems.

a 14 – 7 = _____

b 16 – 9 = _____

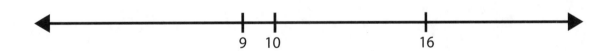

c 13 – 6 = _____

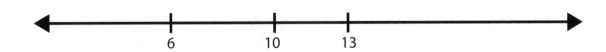

d 14 – 8 = _____

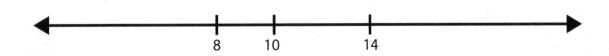

(continued on next page)

71

NAME _____ | DATE _____

Subtracting on the Line & Solving Story Problems page 2 of 2

2 Jose, Matt, and Dani went to the library. They each checked out 5 books. How many books is that in all? Show your work.

Jose, Matt, and Dani checked out _____ books in all.

3 **CHALLENGE** Show your work on each problem. Four granola bars cost $2.00.

a How much does 1 granola bar cost? _____

b How much do 2 granola bars cost? _____

c How much do 5 granola bars cost? _____

NAME | DATE

 Family Age Number Line page 1 of 2

Note to Families

Students have been learning how to use the number line to solve subtraction problems. In this assignment, your child will use a length of adding machine tape to make a number line that shows the ages of some of the people in your family, and then use the number line to solve some problems.

Materials

- Family Age Number Line, pages 1–2
- length of adding machine tape (brought home from school)
- pencil and crayons or colored markers

Making the Number Line

1 In the table below, write the names and ages of 5 to 7 family members. This can include children, adults, grandparents, cousins, aunts, uncles, or even pets.

Name	Age

2 Now write the ages you listed above in order, from youngest to oldest, on the lines below. (There are 7 lines, but you only have to use as many as you need.)

_____ , _____ , _____ , _____ , _____ , _____ , _____

least   greatest

3 Get the length of adding machine tape you brought home. Write a 0 at the far left side and the age of the oldest person you listed on the right side. Here is an example.

0	67

4 Now write the rest of the ages you listed where they belong on the adding machine tape.

(continued on next page)

Family Age Number Line page 2 of 2

Solving Problems on the Number Line

5 Use your adding machine tape number line to help figure out the difference between the oldest and youngest person on your list. Show the strategy you used on the open number line below. Then write your answer.

The oldest person on my family list is _____ years older than the youngest person on my family list.

6 Choose an adult in your family and use the adding machine tape number line to help figure out the difference between your age and the adult family member's age. Show the strategy you used on the open number line below. Then write your answer.

My family member is _____ years older than I am.

7 Timmy is 8. His dad is 32. Use hops on the open number line below to find out how much older Timmy's dad is than Timmy. Then fill in the missing numbers in the equations below.

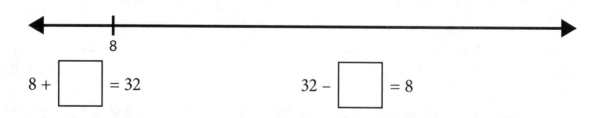

8

$8 + \boxed{} = 32$ $32 - \boxed{} = 8$

8 **CHALLENGE** Why does the same number work in both of the equations above?

NAME _____ | DATE _____

🏠 Adding, Counting & Solving Problems page 1 of 2

1 Fill in the missing numbers to complete the addition facts.

$5 + 5 =$ _____ $4 + 4 =$ _____ $2 + 2 =$ _____

$8 +$ _____ $= 16$ $9 +$ _____ $= 18$ _____ $+ 6 = 12$

_____ $+ 3 = 6$ $10 + 2 =$ _____ $6 + 10 =$ _____

$3 +$ _____ $= 13$ $10 +$ _____ $= 18$ $8 +$ _____ $= 16$

2 Fill in the missing numbers to complete the pattern.

a Skip-count forward by 5s

5, 10, 15, _____, 25, _____, _____

b Skip-count forward by 5s

40, _____, 50, _____, _____, 65

c Skip-count forward by 5s

13, 18, 23, _____, 33, _____, _____

d Skip-count forward by 5s

19, 24, _____, 34, 39, _____, 49

e Skip-count backward by 5s.

30, 25, _____, 15, _____, _____

f Skip-count backward by 5s.

27, 22, _____, 12, _____, _____

3 **CHALLENGE** Skip-count by 5s. Circle the word to show whether you went forward or backward each time.

a 143, 138, 133, _____, 123, _____, 113, _____, _____, 98   forward   backward

b 332, 337, 342, _____, 352, 357, _____, _____, 372, _____   forward   backward

c 488, 493, 498, _____, _____, 513, _____, _____, _____, 533   forward   backward

d 267, 262, 257, _____, _____, _____, 237, _____, 227, _____   forward   backward

(continued on next page)

Adding, Counting & Solving Problems page 2 of 2

4 Mrs. Brown is the gym teacher. She has 15 soccer balls and 8 footballs.

   a How many more soccer balls than footballs does Mrs. Brown have? Show your work.

        Mrs. Brown has _____ more soccer balls than footballs.

   b How many soccer balls and footballs does Mrs. Brown have in all? Show your work.

        Mrs. Brown has _____ soccer balls and footballs in all.

5 CHALLENGE Jason had 2 quarters and 1 dime. He went to the school store to spend all his money. What 3 things could he buy? Find at least 2 different answers. Show your work.

School Store Price List	
Markers	$0.25 each
Tablets	$0.30 each
Erasers	$0.10 each
Pencils	$0.20 each
Folders	$0.15 each

       76

NAME _____ | DATE _____

🏠 Tens & Ones, Nuts & Carrots page 1 of 2

1 Tell how many tens and ones there are in each set of base ten pieces. Then write an equation to show the total.

ex	10s	1s
	3	6
	Equation	
	30 + 6 = 36	

a	10s	1s
	Equation	

b	10s	1s
	Equation	

c	10s	1s
	Equation	

d	10s	1s
	Equation	

2 Tell how many dimes and pennies there are in each box. Then write an equation to show the total.

ex	Dimes	Pennies
	2	1
	Equation	
	20¢ + 1¢ = 21¢	

a	Dimes	Pennies
	Equation	

b	Dimes	Pennies
	Equation	

c	Dimes	Pennies
	Equation	

d	Dimes	Pennies
	Equation	

(continued on next page)

NAME _____ | DATE _____

Tens & Ones, Nuts & Carrots page 2 of 2

3 The squirrels are hiding nuts for the winter. Three of the squirrels each got 4 nuts. Five of the squirrels each got 5 nuts. How many nuts do they have in all? Show your work.

The squirrels got _____ nuts in all.

4 **CHALLENGE** The zookeeper brought 9 bunches of carrots for the elephants. Each bunch had 5 carrots. He gave one of the elephants 24 carrots. How many carrots were left for the other elephants? Show your work.

There were_____ carrots left for the other elephants.

78

NAME _____ **| DATE** _____

Shopping & Adding page 1 of 2

1 Erika went to the store. She got a pencil for 15¢ and a tablet for 25¢. She gave the storekeeper 50¢. How much money did she get back? Show your work.

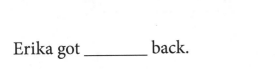
Erika got _____ back.

2 **CHALLENGE** Use the numbers in the box to solve the problems below.

15	24	6	8	3	17	4	20	32	10

a Find 2 numbers whose sum is 40. _____ _____

b Find 2 numbers whose sum is 18. _____ _____

c Find 2 other numbers whose sum is 18. _____ _____

d Find 2 numbers whose difference is 12. _____ _____

e Find 3 numbers that have the largest total. _____ _____ _____

f What is the total of those 3 numbers? Show your work.

(continued on next page)

NAME | **DATE**

Shopping & Adding page 2 of 2

3 Add. Use the pictures of base ten pieces to help. The second set of pieces for each problem is hidden, so you will have to draw them or imagine them.

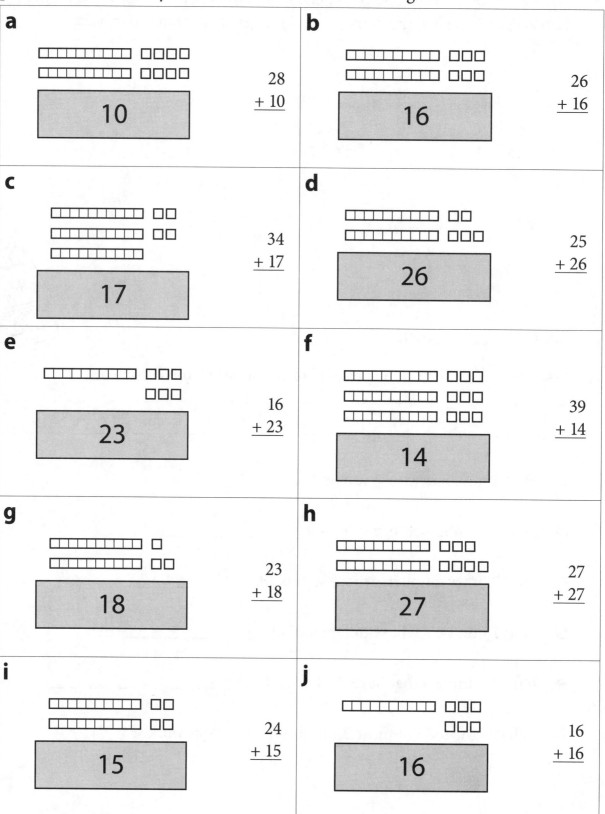

a
10
$\begin{array}{r} 28 \\ + 10 \\ \hline \end{array}$

b
16
$\begin{array}{r} 26 \\ + 16 \\ \hline \end{array}$

c
17
$\begin{array}{r} 34 \\ + 17 \\ \hline \end{array}$

d
26
$\begin{array}{r} 25 \\ + 26 \\ \hline \end{array}$

e
23
$\begin{array}{r} 16 \\ + 23 \\ \hline \end{array}$

f
14
$\begin{array}{r} 39 \\ + 14 \\ \hline \end{array}$

g
18
$\begin{array}{r} 23 \\ + 18 \\ \hline \end{array}$

h
27
$\begin{array}{r} 27 \\ + 27 \\ \hline \end{array}$

i
15
$\begin{array}{r} 24 \\ + 15 \\ \hline \end{array}$

j
16
$\begin{array}{r} 16 \\ + 16 \\ \hline \end{array}$

80

Solving Presents & Parcels Story Problems page 1 of 2

Note to Families

Your student has spent the last several days at school working to create and solve story problems about presents and groups of 10 presents called parcels. As students work on this Home Connection, ask them to show you how working in groups of 10 rather than counting by 1s can make their work faster. You may even choose to work alongside your student and share some of your strategies to arrive at the same answer.

Solving Presents & Parcels Story Problems

Read the presents and parcels story problems on this sheet and the next, and choose at least four you want to solve. Then go to work. Remember—the answer is not enough. You need to show how you solved each problem, using pictures, numbers, and/or words. Be sure to work in 10s instead of 1s whenever you can.

ex Emile is having a birthday party. There are 35 presents for Emile at the party. Some of the presents are in the closet, and 19 of the presents are on the table. How many presents are in the closet?

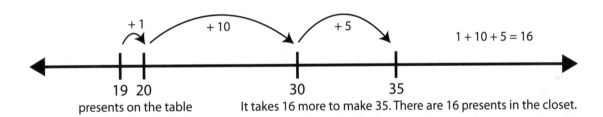

1 It was June 29, Vincent's birthday. There were 12 presents on the fireplace and 23 on the table. How many presents in all?

2 It was Jake and Sam's birthday. There were 26 presents. Jake and Sam wanted to split them evenly, but they didn't know how. Can you help them?

(continued on next page)

NAME | **DATE**

Solving Presents & Parcels Story Problems page 2 of 2

3 It was April 24, my sister's birthday. Six kids came to her party. She had it at Zippy's Pizza. Each kid brought 10 presents. My mom gave her 2 presents. How many presents did she get in all?

4 Today is Briana's 18th birthday. She knows there are 18 presents in the closet and also 23 presents under the table. Now Briana wants to know how many in all.

5 Dan was having a Valentine's party. There were 24 presents in the closet and 23 on the table. Then someone opened 12 of the presents. How many were not yet opened?

6 It was Jessie's big party. Jessie said to come at 5:00 PM. One of his friends peeked through the window. He saw only 13 presents. Jessie said there were supposed to be 42 presents. How many presents were in the closet?

7 **CHALLENGE** It was Taylor's 8th birthday and there were 47 presents. Each kid brought 10 presents, except for 3 kids who brought 5 presents each and 2 kids who brought 1 present each. How many kids came to Taylor's party?

Shopping & Subtracting page 1 of 2

1 Alex went to the store. She bought an orange for 25¢, an apple for 24¢, and a banana for 23¢. How much money did she spend in all? Show your work.

Alex spent _____ in all.

2 **CHALLENGE** Jake has 3 quarters and 4 nickels. An apple costs 20¢. How many apples can Jake buy? Show your work.

Jake can buy _____ apples.

(continued on next page)

NAME |DATE

Shopping & Subtracting page 2 of 2

3 Subtract. Use the pictures of base ten pieces to help.

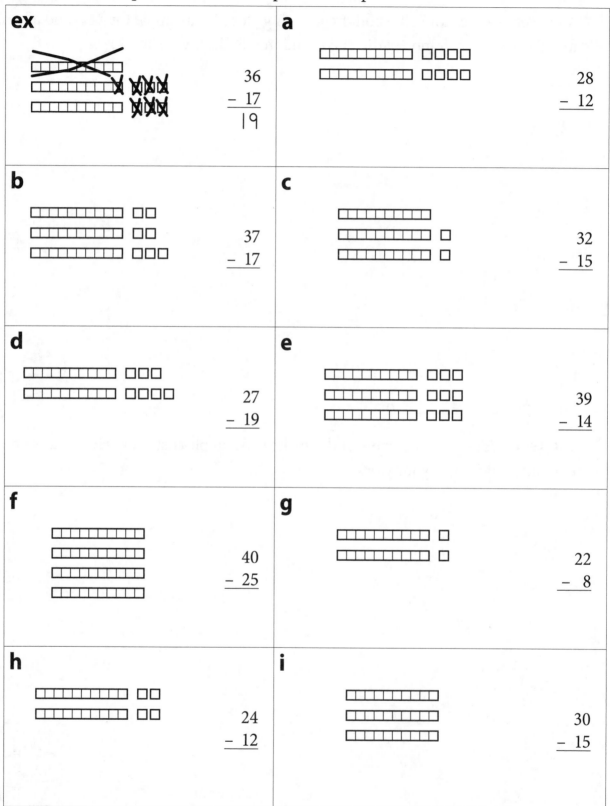

ex	a
36 − 17 19	28 − 12
b 37 − 17	**c** 32 − 15
d 27 − 19	**e** 39 − 14
f 40 − 25	**g** 22 − 8
h 24 − 12	**i** 30 − 15

84

Sorting & Graphing a Collection page 1 of 3

Note to Families

One of the mathematical topics we study in second grade is data analysis—collecting, graphing, and interpreting data. In this Home Connection, your child gets to organize and present information about one of his or her collections, or about a collection you have around the home. There are many sets of things that would work: rocks, shells, buttons, toy cars, stamps, books, cans of food, Legos, and so on. The only requirement is that there be 30 or more items in the collection and that there is enough variation in the items so they can be sorted in several different ways.

Sorting a Collection

Find a collection of some type around your home. It can be almost anything—rocks, shells, action figures, buttons, nuts and bolts, crayons, sports cards, etc. The collection you use for this assignment should have somewhere between 30 and 100 items. Once you've decided on your collection, work with someone in your family to sort it in as many ways as you can. List your ideas on the next page.

Here's an example: Suppose I decide to sort my collection of toy cars. I could sort them by 2-door and 4-door, as I have in this picture. (I didn't have room to show all 30!) I could also sort them by color, size, make, or type. See if you can think of at least 5 different ways to sort your collection.

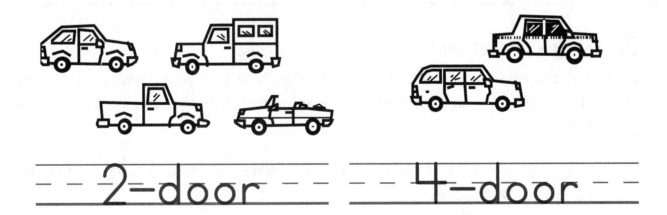

(continued on next page)

NAME | **DATE**

Sorting & Graphing a Collection page 2 of 3

Here's what I collected:

Here's how many there were in my collection:

Here are some ways we sorted the things in my collection:

_____   _____
_ _ _ _ _ _ _ _ _ _ _ _   _ _ _ _ _ _ _ _ _ _ _ _
_____   _____
_ _ _ _ _ _ _ _ _ _ _ _   _ _ _ _ _ _ _ _ _ _ _ _
_____   _____
_ _ _ _ _ _ _ _ _ _ _ _   _ _ _ _ _ _ _ _ _ _ _ _
_____   _____
_ _ _ _ _ _ _ _ _ _ _ _   _ _ _ _ _ _ _ _ _ _ _ _
_____   _____

Graphing a Collection

Look at all the ways you just sorted your collection. Now pick your favorite and make a graph about it on the back of this sheet. Here are some things to remember as you make your graph:

1 You don't have to mark all the columns if you don't need them, but be sure to label each column that you use.

2 If you have more than 10 items in any group, you'll have to make your graphing boxes stand for more than 1. It's okay to have each box stand for 2, 5, or even 10, depending on how many things you have to graph. Just remember to write your numbers in the boxes up the side so that we know how much each stands for.

3 Be sure to give your graph a title so that we understand what it's about.

(continued on next page)

NAME | DATE

Sorting & Graphing a Collection page 3 of 3

Graph Title _____

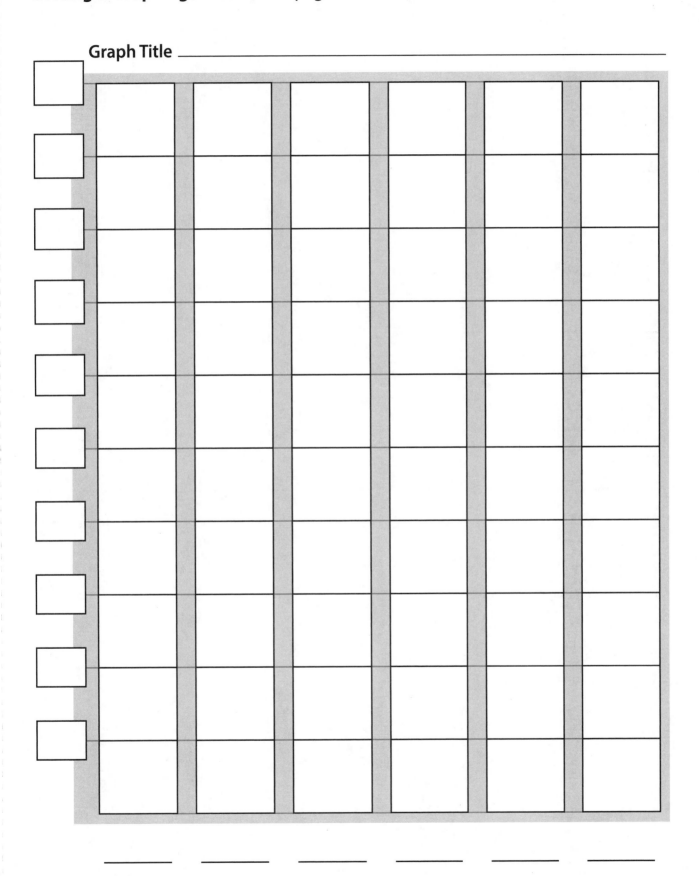

© The Math Learning Center | mathlearningcenter.org

Pencil Puppy & Pal page 1 of 2

1 Fill in the bubble next to the correct answer to each question.

a The number on Pencil Puppy's dog tag has a 6 in the tens place. It has a 4 in the ones place. What is the number on her tag?

     ○ 46   ○ 64   ○ 14   ○ 67

b The number on Pal's dog tag has a 7 in the tens place. It has a 3 in the ones place. What is the number on Pal's tag?

     ○ 17   ○ 37   ○ 30   ○ 73

2 Fill in the correct answer.

a Pencil Puppy's house number has a 3 in the tens place.
It has a 5 in the ones place.
What is Pencil Puppy's house number? _____

b Pal's house number has a 7 in the ones place.
It has a 4 in the tens place.
What is Pal's house number? _____

3 Pencil Puppy has 43 pencils in her house. Pal has 29 pencils in his house. How many pencils do they have in all? Use numbers, pictures, and/or words to solve the problem and explain your answer.

Pencil Puppy and Pal have _____ pencils in all.

(continued on next page)

Pencil Puppy & Pal page 2 of 2

4 Add. Use the pictures of base ten pieces to help. The second set of pieces for each problem is hidden, so you will have to draw them or imagine them.

a		**b**	
base ten pieces	36 + 26	base ten pieces	39 + 14
26		14	

5 When Pencil Puppy does 2-digit addition, she adds the tens first. Next, she adds the ones. Then she adds the two numbers to get the answer. Try her strategy.

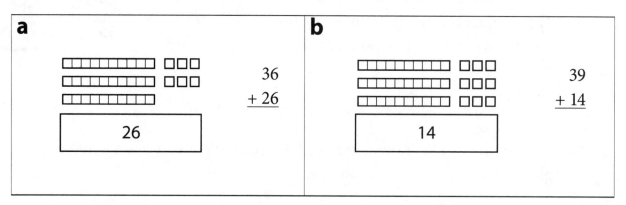

ex

Tens	Ones
3	7
2	7

$30 + 20 = \underline{50}$
$7 + 7 = \underline{14}$
$50 + 14 = \underline{64}$

a

Tens	Ones
4	8
3	4

$40 + 30 = \underline{}$
$8 + 4 = \underline{}$
$70 + 12 = \underline{}$

b

Tens	Ones
5	8
2	8

$50 + 20 = \underline{}$
$8 + 8 = \underline{}$
$70 + 16 = \underline{}$

c

Tens	Ones
2	5
6	9

$20 + 60 = \underline{}$
$5 + 9 = \underline{}$
$\underline{} + \underline{} = \underline{}$

d

Tens	Ones
3	4
5	9

$30 + 50 = \underline{}$
$4 + 9 = \underline{}$
$\underline{} + \underline{} = \underline{}$

e

Tens	Ones
4	5
4	6

$40 + 40 = \underline{}$
$5 + 6 = \underline{}$
$\underline{} + \underline{} = \underline{}$

🏠 Subtraction & Graphing Practice page 1 of 2

DJ Hopper makes hops on the number line to solve 2-digit subtraction problems.

Here's how he solved 53 – 26:

- Start at 26.
- Hop up to 30.
- Now hop up to 50.
- Then hop up to 53 and add up all your hops. That tells how far it is from 26 to 53.

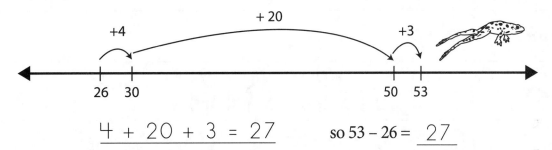

$$4 + 20 + 3 = 27 \qquad \text{so } 53 - 26 = \underline{27}$$

1 Try DJ's number line strategy to solve these subtraction problems.

a 45 – 17

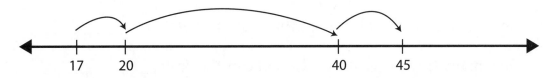

_____ so 45 – 17 = _____

b 54 – 25

_____ so 54 – 25 = _____

c 57 – 18

_____ so 57 – 18 = _____

(continued on next page)

NAME _____ | **DATE** _____

Subtraction & Graphing Practice page 2 of 2

Favorite Pets

2 The second graders in Ms. Nelson's class made a graph with pictures to show their favorite pets. Each student put one picture on the graph to show his or her favorite pet. Use their graph to help answer the questions below.

Our Favorite Pets	
Fish	🐟🐟🐟🐟🐟
Birds	🐦🐦
Cats	🐱🐱🐱🐱🐱🐱🐱🐱
Dogs	🐕🐕🐕🐕🐕🐕🐕🐕🐕🐕🐕🐕

a Which pet did most kids like the best? _____

b How many more kids like dogs than fish the best? _____

c How many fewer kids like birds than cats the best? _____

d Write an equation to show how many kids put pictures on this graph.

3 The kids in Ms. Nelson's class did a survey of all the second grades to find out about kids' favorite pets. Use their chart to help answer the questions below.

a How many more kids like fish than birds the best? Show your work.

2nd Grade Favorite Pets	
Pets	**Number of Kids**
Fish	17
Birds	8
Cats	45
Dogs	62

b How many more kids like dogs than cats the best? Show your work.

Inchworm's Garden & Fives Practice page 1 of 2

Here is Little Inchworm's Garden. Use the inch side of your ruler to measure the path between each part of the garden. Write your answers on the chart below.

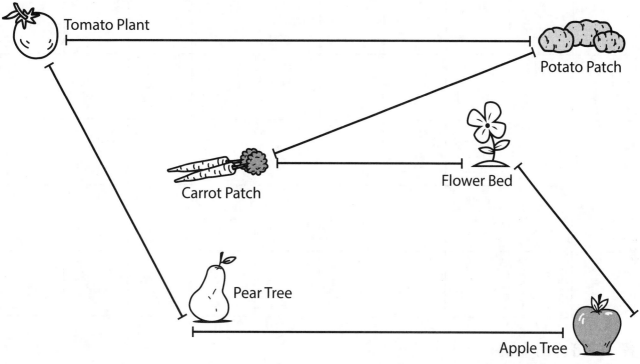

	From	**To**	**How Many Inches?**
1			
2			
3			
4			
5			
6			

(continued on next page)

Inchworm's Garden & Fives Practice page 2 of 2

7 Fill in the missing numbers. Then color in the count-by-5s numbers, starting with 5 (5, 10, 15, 20, and so on).

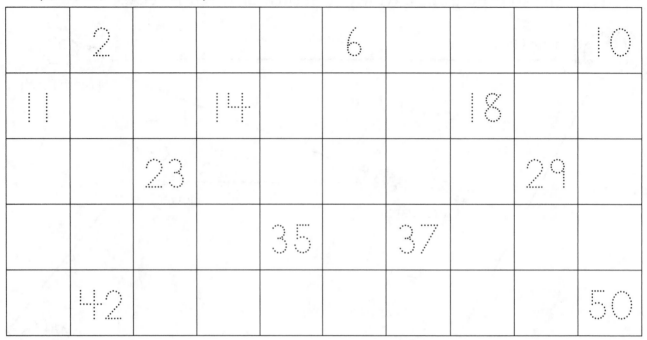

8 Find each sum.

5 + 5 = _____   15 + 5 = _____   21 + 5 = _____   34 + 5 = _____

9 Find each difference.

20 – 5 = _____   15 – 5 = _____   35 – 5 = _____   50 – 5 = _____

10 Fill in the missing numbers on the number line below.

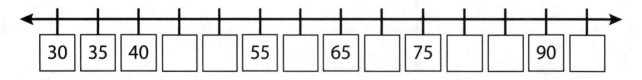

11 What's next in this skip-counting pattern?

1, 6, 11, 16, _____, _____, _____, _____

NAME _____ | **DATE** _____

 Paths & Piggybanks page 1 of 2

Little Inchworm wants to get from the house to the duck pond. She can use Path A, B, or C.

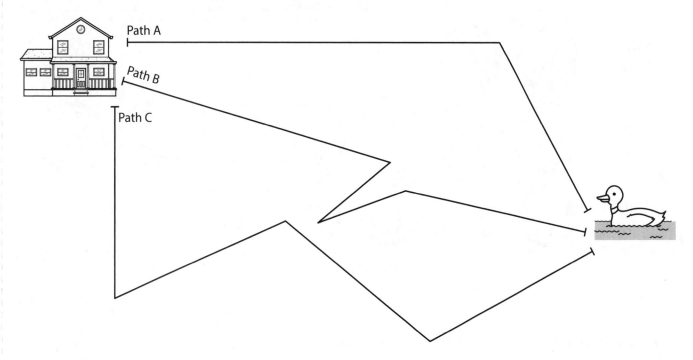

1 Which path looks shortest? (circle one)

Path A   Path B   Path C

2 Use the inch side of your ruler. Measure each path to find out which one is shortest.

a Path A is _____ inches long.

b Path B is _____ inches long.

c Path C is _____ inches long.

3 Which path is shortest? _____

4 Which path is longest? _____

5 **CHALLENGE** Use a red pencil or marker. Draw the shortest path from the house to the duck pond. Measure your new path with the inch side of your ruler.

About how long is your new path? _____ inches

(continued on next page)

95

NAME _____ | DATE _____

Paths & Piggybanks page 2 of 2

Ella took all the coins out of her piggy bank. She made a graph about them.

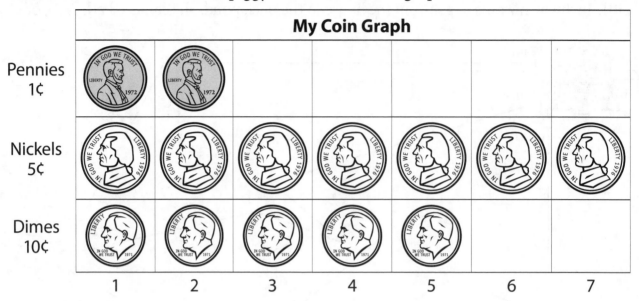

6 Does Ella have more dimes or more pennies? _____

7 Which coin does Ella have the most of? _____

8 How many fewer dimes are there than nickels? _____

9 How much money does Ella have in her bank? _____

10 CHALLENGE Ella wants to buy a binder for $1.00. How much more money does she need? Show your work.

Adding, Subtracting & Measuring page 1 of 2

Hundreds Grid

1	2	3	4	5	6	7	8	9	10
11	12	13	14	15	16	17	18	19	20
21	22	23	24	25	26	27	28	29	30
31	32	33	34	35	36	37	38	39	40
41	42	43	44	45	46	47	48	49	50
51	52	53	54	55	56	57	58	59	60
61	62	63	64	65	66	67	68	69	70
71	72	73	74	75	76	77	78	79	80
81	82	83	84	85	86	87	88	89	90
91	92	93	94	95	96	97	98	99	100

1   Find each sum. Use the hundreds grid to help.

$$\begin{array}{r} 50 \\ + 10 \\ \hline \end{array} \qquad \begin{array}{r} 38 \\ + 10 \\ \hline \end{array} \qquad \begin{array}{r} 45 \\ + 10 \\ \hline \end{array} \qquad \begin{array}{r} 66 \\ + 10 \\ \hline \end{array} \qquad \begin{array}{r} 79 \\ + 10 \\ \hline \end{array} \qquad \begin{array}{r} 53 \\ + 10 \\ \hline \end{array} \qquad \begin{array}{r} 26 \\ + 10 \\ \hline \end{array}$$

$$\begin{array}{r} 19 \\ + 10 \\ \hline \end{array} \qquad \begin{array}{r} 21 \\ + 10 \\ \hline \end{array} \qquad \begin{array}{r} 81 \\ + 10 \\ \hline \end{array} \qquad \begin{array}{r} 37 \\ + 10 \\ \hline \end{array} \qquad \begin{array}{r} 40 \\ + 10 \\ \hline \end{array} \qquad \begin{array}{r} 72 \\ + 10 \\ \hline \end{array} \qquad \begin{array}{r} 27 \\ + 10 \\ \hline \end{array}$$

2   Find each difference. Use the hundreds grid to help.

$$\begin{array}{r} 75 \\ - 10 \\ \hline \end{array} \qquad \begin{array}{r} 55 \\ - 10 \\ \hline \end{array} \qquad \begin{array}{r} 42 \\ - 10 \\ \hline \end{array} \qquad \begin{array}{r} 99 \\ - 10 \\ \hline \end{array} \qquad \begin{array}{r} 87 \\ - 10 \\ \hline \end{array} \qquad \begin{array}{r} 18 \\ - 10 \\ \hline \end{array} \qquad \begin{array}{r} 21 \\ - 10 \\ \hline \end{array}$$

$$\begin{array}{r} 47 \\ - 10 \\ \hline \end{array} \qquad \begin{array}{r} 14 \\ - 10 \\ \hline \end{array} \qquad \begin{array}{r} 51 \\ - 10 \\ \hline \end{array} \qquad \begin{array}{r} 39 \\ - 10 \\ \hline \end{array} \qquad \begin{array}{r} 28 \\ - 10 \\ \hline \end{array} \qquad \begin{array}{r} 77 \\ - 10 \\ \hline \end{array} \qquad \begin{array}{r} 94 \\ - 10 \\ \hline \end{array}$$

(continued on next page)

97

Adding, Subtracting & Measuring page 2 of 2

3 Use a ruler marked in inches to measure each strip. Write the length in the space next to the strip. Label your answers with the correct units (inches, in., or ″).

Strip	Length
a ██████████████	
b █████████	
c ███████████	
d ███████████████	

4 There are 12 inches in 1 foot. Use this information to answer the questions below.

a How many feet are equal to 24 inches? _____

b How many feet are equal to 36 inches? _____

5 Rodney has a piece of rope that is 82 inches long. Simon has a piece of rope that is 27 inches long. How much longer is Rodney's piece of rope? Show all your work.

6 **CHALLENGE** Maria and Katy each have a piece of string. When they put the two pieces of string together end to end, the total length is 84 inches. Maria's string is 6 inches longer than Katy's. How long is Maria's piece of string? How long is Katy's piece of string? Show all your work. Use another piece of paper if you need to.

NAME _____ | **DATE** _____

🏠 Subtraction Facts & Coin Problems page 1 of 2

1 Complete the problems below.

a Circle all the Subtract 2 facts in blue. Then find each difference.
(example 10 – 2 or 16 – 2)

b Circle all the Subtract Half facts in red. Then find each difference.
(example 12 – 6 or 14 – 7)

c Circle all the Take Away Ten facts in green. Then find each difference.
(example 14 – 10 or 19 – 10)

d Circle all the Back to Ten facts in purple. Then find each difference.
(example 13 – 3 or 17 – 7)

e And now—see if you can use the facts you've circled and solved to help you
figure out the rest!

15 – 2	14 – 6	13 – 3	10 – 2	14 – 7	14 – 8	19 – 9
15 – 5	17 – 8	17 – 10	11 – 2	16 – 8	18 – 8	19 – 2
18 – 9	10 – 5	18 – 4	19 – 10	13 – 2	14 – 4	11 – 5
16 – 9	14 – 10	12 – 10	16 – 10	14 – 2	12 – 4	20 – 5
120 – 60	83 – 10	140 – 70	160 – 80	29 – 2	180 – 90	48 – 8

(continued on next page)

99

Subtraction Facts & Coin Problems page 2 of 2

2 Sara has four coins in her right pocket. Together, they are worth 30¢. What four coins does Sara have in her right pocket? Show your work.

The four coins Sara has in her right pocket are

3 Sara has seven coins in her left pocket. Together, they are worth 24¢. What seven coins does Sara have in her left pocket? Show your work.

The seven coins Sara has in her left pocket are

Computation & Story Problems page 1 of 2

1 Find each sum.

9	9	10	9	10	9	9
+ 6	+ 9	+ 7	+ 7	+ 6	+ 10	+ 4

9	10	11	8	4	9	2
+ 3	+ 7	+ 9	+ 9	+ 10	+ 5	+ 9

20	40	30	60	30	90	80
+ 9	+ 12	+ 8	+ 15	+ 17	+ 8	+ 14

20	32	58	62	40	70	75
+ 29	+ 20	+ 30	+ 20	+ 39	+ 23	+ 10

2 Find each difference.

16	16	13	13	18	18	20
− 10	− 9	− 10	− 9	− 10	− 9	− 10

50	40	30	60	70	90	80
− 10	− 20	− 10	− 40	− 30	− 40	− 60

26	35	78	64	55	38	58
− 10	− 10	− 20	− 30	− 40	− 20	− 20

(continued on next page)

Computation & Story Problems page 2 of 2

3 Sawyer is preparing a salad for dinner. He has 17 radishes and 8 tomatoes.

a How many more radishes than tomatoes does Sawyer have?
Show your work.

Sawyer has _____ more radishes than tomatoes.

b How many radishes and tomatoes does Sawyer have in all?
Show your work.

Sawyer has _____ radishes and tomatoes in all.

4 Chanel went to the craft store with 3 quarters and 2 dimes. She bought three different things from the list below. What three things might she have bought? Find at least two different answers. Show your work.

Craft Store Price List	
Brushes	$0.60 each
Art Cards	$0.50 each
Erasers	$0.10 each
Mini-Pencils	$0.25 each
Envelopes	$0.35 each

NAME _____ |**DATE** _____

🏠 **Math with Pencil Puppy** page 1 of 2

1 Add. Use the pictures of base ten pieces to help. The second set of pieces for each problem is hidden, so you will have to draw them or imagine them.

a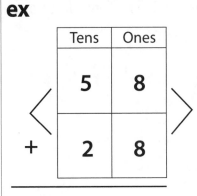

28
+ 13

b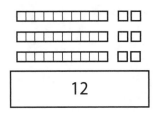

36
+ 12

2 Find each sum.

70 + 8 = _____   40 + 7 = _____   30 + 16 = _____   20 + 13 = _____

3 Use Pencil Puppy's strategy for adding 2-digit numbers. Remember, she adds the tens first. Then she adds the ones. Then she finds the total.

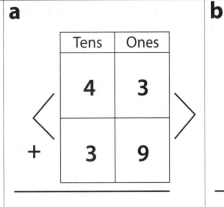

ex

Tens	Ones
5	8
2	8

<   >

+

_____ + _____ = _____

a

Tens	Ones
4	3
3	9

<   >

+

_____ + _____ = _____

b

Tens	Ones
2	7
4	5

<   >

+

_____ + _____ = _____

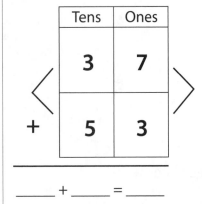

c

Tens	Ones
1	6
2	2

<   >

+

_____ + _____ = _____

d

Tens	Ones
3	7
5	3

<   >

+

_____ + _____ = _____

e

Tens	Ones
3	3
5	8

<   >

+

_____ + _____ = _____

(continued on next page)

NAME _____ | **DATE** _____

Math with Pencil Puppy page 2 of 2

4 Jen had some flowers. Her friend gave her 9 more flowers. Now she has 14 flowers. How many flowers did Jen have to start with? Show your work.

Jen had _____ flowers to start with.

5 **CHALLENGE** Jon had 4 oranges. He cut each orange into 8 slices. How many orange slices did he have in all? Show your work.

Jon had _____ orange slices in all.

NAME _____ | **DATE** _____

🏠 Two-Digit Subtraction & Story Problems page 1 of 2

Use DJ's number line strategy to solve these subtraction problems.

ex 64 – 35

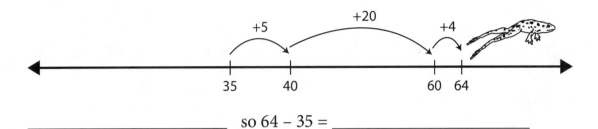

_____ so 64 – 35 = _____

1 60 – 32

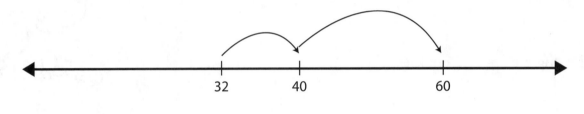

_____ so 60 – 32 = _____

2 54 – 27

_____ so 54 – 27 = _____

3 71 – 26

_____ so 71 – 26 = _____

(continued on next page)

NAME | **DATE**

Two-Digit Subtraction & Story Problems page 2 of 2

4 There were 15 cookies on the plate. The dog ate some of them. Now there are only 7 cookies on the plate. How many did the dog eat? Show your work.

The dog ate _____ cookies.

5 Ann had 4 apples. She cut each apple into 5 slices. Each slice had 3 seeds in it. How many seeds in all? Show your work.

There were _____ seeds in all.

Patterns with Numbers & Beads page 1 of 2

1 Fill in the missing numbers on this chart.

1	2		4	5	6	7	8	9	10
11	12	13		15	16		18	19	20
21		23	24	25		27	28	29	30
	32	33	34	35	36	37	38		40
41	42		44	45	46	47		49	
51		53	54		56	57	58	59	60
	62	63	64	65		67	68		70
71	72		74	75	76		78	79	
81	82	83		85	86	87		89	90
91		93	94		96	97	98	99	100

a Color all the counting-by-2s numbers red.

b Color all the counting-by-5s numbers yellow.

c Color all the counting-by-10s numbers blue.

2 The numbers in the box are mixed up! Put them in order from least to greatest.

62	51	17	78	40	14

_____ , _____ , _____ , _____ , _____ , _____

least   greatest

(continued on next page)

NAME | **DATE**

Patterns with Numbers & Beads page 2 of 2

3 Trina has 17 beads. Nine of the beads are blue, and the rest are red.

a How many red beads does Trina have? Show your work.

Trina has _____ red beads.

b Trina wants to make a bracelet with her beads. How can she make a color pattern with her 17 blue and red beads? Draw a picture to show.

4 **CHALLENGE** Look for a pattern. Fill in the missing numbers that fit your pattern.

a 1, 7, 13, 19, _____, _____, _____,

b 2, 7, 12, 17, _____, _____, _____, 37, _____, _____, 52

c 25, 20, 15, _____, _____, _____

d 24, 20, 16, 12, _____, _____, _____

e 1, 2, 4, 7, 11, _____, _____, 29, _____, 46, _____

f 1, 2, 4, 8, _____, _____, _____, 128, _____, _____

NAME _____ | DATE _____

 Extra Facts page 1 of 2

1 Find the sum.

80	30	44	50	70	51	60
+ 6	+ 43	+ 24	+ 38	+ 7	+ 17	+ 16

370	120	890	360	340	430	125
+ 8	+ 6	+ 4	+ 15	+ 50	+ 27	+ 25

2 Use pictures, numbers, and/or words to find the sum in each box. Show all your work.

a 36 + 55	**b** 129 + 133

3 Find the difference.

86	39	48	56	35	55	50
– 6	– 9	– 7	– 5	– 15	– 25	– 25

4 Use pictures, numbers, and/or words to find the difference. Show all your work.

51 – 26 =

(continued on next page)

NAME _____ | **DATE** _____

Extra Facts page 2 of 2

Sometimes story problems give you more facts than you need to solve the problem. In each problem below, cross out the fact you don't need. Then solve the problem. Show your work.

5 Nick has 3 cats. He had 12 fish. He gave 4 of the fish to his friend. How many fish does he have left?

Nick has _____ fish left.

6 Lin's big sister is 15. She listened to 8 songs on her music player in the morning. She listened to 9 more songs that night. How many songs did she listen to in all?

Lin's big sister listened to _____ songs in all.

7 Amber made 9 cupcakes. Then she made 12 more cupcakes. It took 2 cups of sugar to make the frosting. How many cupcakes did she make in all?

Amber made _____ cupcakes in all.

8 **CHALLENGE** The Green Dragon had 250 gold pieces. He is 18 feet tall. He is mad because the trolls took 60 of his gold pieces. How many gold pieces does he have left?

The Green Dragon has _____ gold pieces left.

Large Numbers page 1 of 2

1 Trace the numerals and the words.

1 one 2 two 3 three
4 four 5 five 6 six
7 seven 8 eight 9 nine
10 ten 20 twenty
30 thirty 40 forty
50 fifty 60 sixty
70 seventy 80 eighty
90 ninety 100 one hundred

2 Label each set of base ten pieces with the correct number name.

ex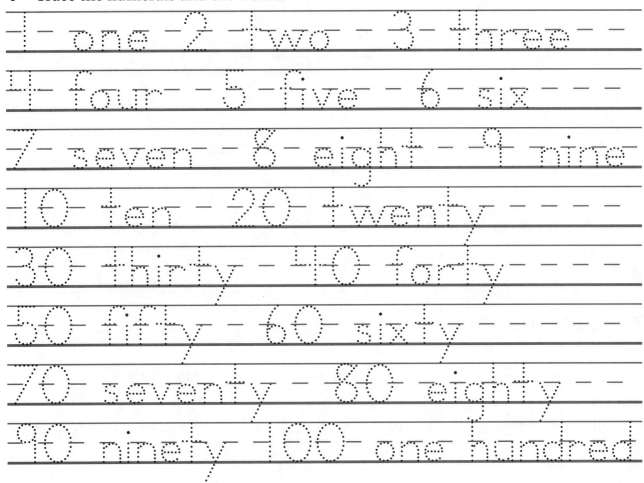

one hundred thirty-two

a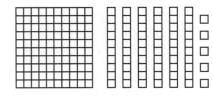

b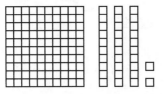

c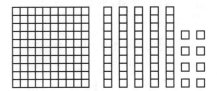

(continued on next page)

NAME _____ | **DATE** _____

Large Numbers page 2 of 2

3 Read each number. Then write it in expanded form.

ex three hundred twenty-nine $329 = 300 + 20 + 9$	**a** four hundred thirty-eight
b two hundred sixteen	**c** five hundred seventy-three
d one hundred ninety-eight	**e** six hundred three
f nine hundred sixty-seven	**g** eight hundred seventeen

4 Find the sum.

$300 + 60 + 5 =$ _____ $500 + 40 + 5 =$ _____ $200 + 10 + 6 =$ _____

$400 + 90 + 9 =$ _____ $100 + 10 + 8 =$ _____ $600 + 7 =$ _____

300	400	600	800	700	100	900
40	20	30	70	80	10	30
+ 5	+ 6	+ 7	+ 8	+ 9	+ 5	+ 6

5 Circle one.

a The **4** in **574** is in the	ones place	tens place	hundreds place
b The **4** in **493** is in the	ones place	tens place	hundreds place
c The **4** in **114** is in the	ones place	tens place	hundreds place
d The **4** in **5,348** is in the	ones place	tens place	hundreds place

NAME | **DATE**

 Thinking About Place Value page 1 of 2

1 Trace the numerals and the words.

1 one 2 two 3 three
4 four 5 five 6 six
7 seven 8 eight 9 nine
10 ten 20 twenty
30 thirty 40 forty
50 fifty 60 sixty
70 seventy 80 eighty
90 ninety 100 one hundred

2 Label each set of base ten pieces with the correct number name.

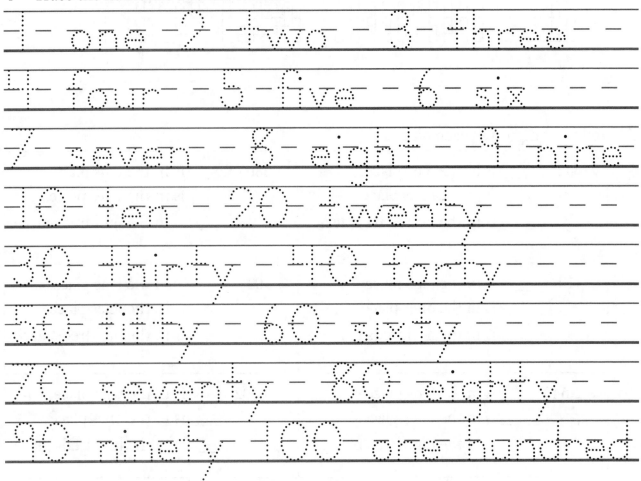

ex

one hundred eighteen

a

b

c

(continued on next page)

NAME _____ | DATE _____

Thinking About Place Value page 2 of 2

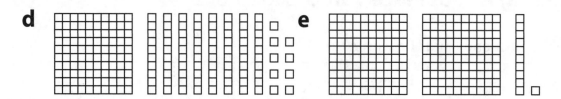

3 Tell what digit is in each place.

a 643 _____ is in the tens place. _____ is in the ones place. _____ is in the hundreds place.	**b** 286 _____ is in the tens place. _____ is in the ones place. _____ is in the hundreds place.
c 119 _____ is in the tens place. _____ is in the ones place. _____ is in the hundreds place.	**d** 903 _____ is in the tens place. _____ is in the ones place. _____ is in the hundreds place.
e 2,643 _____ is in the tens place. _____ is in the ones place. _____ is in the hundreds place.	**f** 5,502 _____ is in the tens place. _____ is in the ones place. _____ is in the hundreds place.

4 **CHALLENGE** Solve these number riddles.

a I have a 9 in the tens place. I have a 4 in the hundreds place. The number in my ones place is less than 3. I am an even number. What number am I? _____	**b** I have a 7 in the thousands place. I have a 0 in the hundreds place. I have a 3 in the tens place. The number in my ones place is greater than 7. I am an odd number. What number am I? _____

NAME _____ **| DATE** _____

 Tens, Nines, Clocks & Coins page 1 of 2

1 Beckett had a quarter in his bank. His mom gave him another quarter for carrying in the groceries, and he found 2 nickels and 3 pennies in the car. How much money did he have in all? Show your work.

Beckett had _____ in all.

2 Willie, Donald, and Maya found a quarter, a dime, a nickel, and 2 pennies when they were cleaning the house. They traded their dad for some other coins that were worth the same amount of money and split up the money evenly. How much did they each get? Show your work.

Willie, Donald, and Maya each got _____.

(continued on next page)

117

NAME | **DATE**

Tens, Nines, Clocks & Coins page 2 of 2

3 Find each sum.

400	400	550	550	780	780	670
+ 10	+ 9	+ 10	+ 9	+ 10	+ 9	+ 20

160	160	720	720	240	240	360
+ 10	+ 9	+ 10	+ 9	+ 30	+ 29	+ 40

4 Find each difference.

300	300	460	460	810	810	430
− 10	− 9	− 10	− 9	− 10	− 9	− 20

350	350	290	290	750	750	680
− 10	− 9	− 10	− 9	− 10	− 9	− 40

5 Read each of these clock faces and write the time on the digital clock.

a   **b**   **c**   **d**

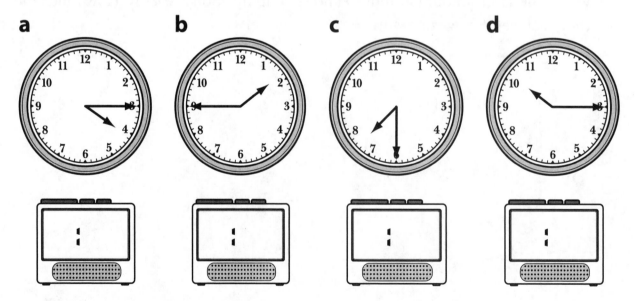

NAME | **DATE**

 Mr. Mole's Money page 1 of 2

1 Mr. Mole digs tunnels every day. Sometimes he finds money buried in the ground. Count the money he found on Monday, Tuesday, and Wednesday. Circle the correct amount in each box.

ex $125

(($1.25))

12.5¢

$12.5

a Monday

$0.60

$6.00

$0.06

$0.75

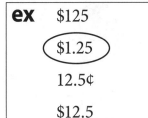

b Tuesday

$3.51

$41.00

5¢

41¢

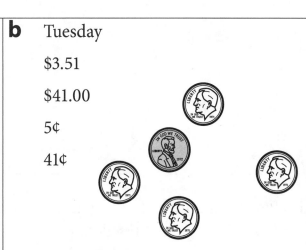

c Wednesday

$3.31

$35.0

$347

$3.47

(continued on next page)

119

NAME | DATE

Mr. Mole's Money page 2 of 2

2 Mr. Mole needs help! He is still a little mixed up about how to use the dollar sign, the cent sign, and the decimal point. Count the money in each box and write the amount correctly.

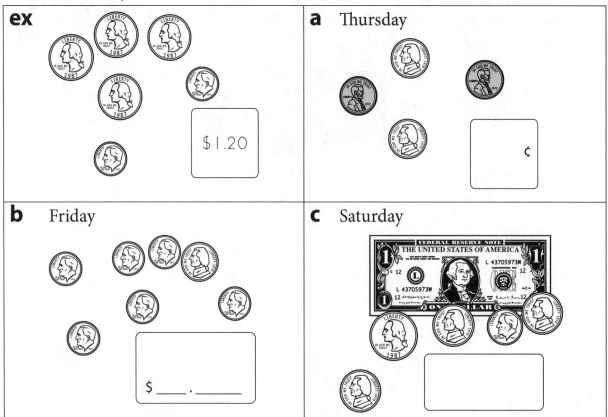

ex $1.20

a Thursday ¢

b Friday $ ____ . ____

c Saturday

3 Put the amounts of money in order from least to greatest on the six lines below. Don't forget to use the dollar sign, the decimal point, and the cents sign wherever you need them.

| $2.50 | 18¢ | 37¢ | $0.72 | $1.47 | $0.03 |

_____ , _____ , _____ , _____ , _____ , _____

least   greatest

4 On Sunday, Mr. Mole found 35¢. Draw three different collections of coins worth $0.35 in the boxes below. (Hint: Use real or plastic coins to help.)

NAME _____ | DATE _____

Money & Time Problems page 1 of 2

If you have an amount of money less than a dollar, you can write the amount with a cents sign or a dollar sign.

1 Count the money in each row, and write it in two different ways.

ex ⬤⬤⬤⬤⬤   _____23¢_____ or _____$0.23_____

a ⬤⬤⬤⬤⬤   _____ or _____

b ⬤⬤⬤⬤⬤   _____ or _____

c ⬤⬤⬤⬤⬤   _____ or _____

2 Write the name of each coin. Show how to write it with a cents sign or a dollar sign. Then draw a different way to make the same amount of money with more than one coin.

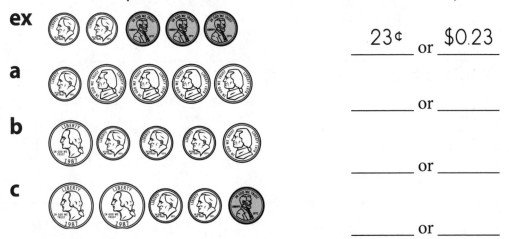

	ex	**a**	**b**
Coin Name	_____nickel_____	_____	_____
Written two ways	5¢		
	$0.05		
Different way to make it.	1¢ 1¢ 1¢ 1¢ 1¢		

(continued on next page)

NAME | **DATE**

Money & Time Problems page 2 of 2

3 Solve these coin problems. You can use quarters, dimes, nickels, and/or pennies.

a Draw 56¢ using 4 coins.	**b** Draw 66¢ using 5 coins.
c Draw 29¢ using 5 coins.	**d** **CHALLENGE** Draw $1.34 using 10 coins.

4 Fill in the bubble next to the correct time.

a

○ 6:15
○ 6:45

b

○ 4:30
○ 3:30

c

○ 2:00
○ 2:15

5 Draw the two hands on the clock to show the time.

a 6:45

b 3:30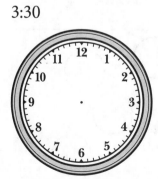

c 7:15

122

NAME _____ | **DATE** _____

 Numbers from 900 to 1,000 page 1 of 2

1 Fill in the missing numbers on the grid below. Use the patterns you know to help.

901		903		905	906	907		909	910
911	912	913	914	915		917	918	919	920
	922	923	924	925	926			929	930
931	932	933		935	936		938	939	940
941		943	944		946	947	948	949	950
951	952	953	954	955		957	958	959	960
961	962	963		965	966	967	968		970
	972	973	974		976	977		979	980
981	982		984	985	986	987	988	989	
991	992	993	994	995		997	998	999	1,000

2 Describe at least three different patterns you see on the grid.

(continued on next page)

123

Numbers from 900 to 1,000 page 2 of 2

3 The carnival in our town started last week. The chart below shows how many tickets they sold each day.

Day	Number of Tickets
Saturday	978 tickets
Sunday	995 tickets
Monday	932 tickets
Tuesday	905 tickets
Wednesday	937 tickets

a Which day did they sell the most tickets? _____

b Which day did they sell the least tickets? _____

c Put the number of tickets they sold each day in order from least to greatest.

_____ , _____ , _____ , _____ , _____

least   greatest

4 The people who came to the carnival bought 909 hot dogs on Saturday, 990 hot dogs on Sunday, 943 hot dogs on Monday, and 934 hot dogs on Tuesday.

a Which is greater, 909 or 990? _____

b How do you know?

c Which is less, 943 or 934? _____

d How do you know?

NAME **|DATE**

 Lines, Buttons & Adding Practice page 1 of 2

1 Find each sum. Use the pictures of base ten pieces to help.

a

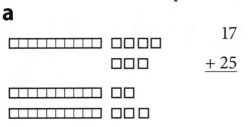

17
+ 25

b

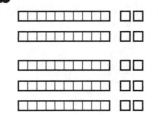

24
+ 36

2 Find each sum.

21 + 8 = _____   42 + 7 = _____   32 + 16 = _____   24 + 13 = _____

3 Use Pencil Puppy's strategy for adding 2-digit numbers. Remember, she adds the tens first. Then she adds the ones. Then she finds the total.

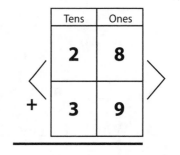

ex	**a**	**b**

ex

	Tens	Ones
	3	7
+	3	4

60 < > 11

60 + 11 = 71

a

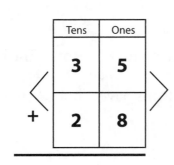

	Tens	Ones
	3	5
+	2	8

___ + ___ = ___

b

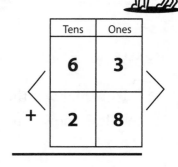

	Tens	Ones
	6	3
+	2	8

___ + ___ = ___

c

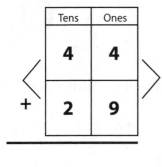

	Tens	Ones
	4	4
+	2	9

___ + ___ = ___

d

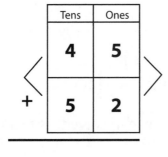

	Tens	Ones
	4	5
+	5	2

___ + ___ = ___

e

	Tens	Ones
	2	8
+	3	9

___ + ___ = ___

(continued on next page)

NAME _____ | DATE _____

Lines, Buttons & Adding Practice page 2 of 2

4 Tami is standing in line. There are 3 other children in front of her. There are 8 children behind her.

a How many children are standing in line? Show your work.

There are _____ children standing in line.

b Which strategy did you use to solve this problem? (Circle one.)

Draw a picture   Make a chart   Write a number sentence   Other

5 **CHALLENGE** Frank's mom gave him 8 buttons. The buttons have 22 holes in all.

a How many of the 8 buttons have 4 holes? How many of the 8 buttons have 2 holes? Show your work.

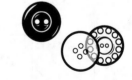

_____ of the 8 buttons have 4 holes. _____ of the 8 buttons have 2 holes.

b Which strategy did you use to solve this problem? (Circle one.)

Draw a picture   Make a chart   Write a number sentence   Other

NAME _____ | DATE _____

🏠 Numbers, Cubes & Marbles page 1 of 2

1 Count by 10s, either forward or backward, to fill in the missing numbers.

a 10, 20, 30, 40, _____, _____, _____, 80, _____, 100, 110, _____, _____

b 280, 270, 260, _____, _____, 230, _____, _____, 200, _____, _____

c 203, 213, 223, _____, _____, 253, _____, _____, _____, 293, _____

d 567, 557, 547, 537, _____, _____, 507, _____, 487, _____, 467

2 Count by 100s, either forward or backward, to fill in the missing numbers.

a 100, 200, 300, _____, _____, _____, 700, _____, _____

b 950, 850, 750, _____, _____, _____, 350, _____, _____

c 203, 303, 403, _____, _____, _____, 803, _____, 1003

d 914, 814, 714, _____, _____, 414, _____, _____, _____

3 Find each sum.

400 + 70 + 2 = _____   600 + 20 + 8 = _____

800 + 50 + 5 = _____   100 + 10 + 3 = _____

200	300	700	200	400	100	900
50	80	40	60	40	10	90
+ 9	+ 1	+ 2	+ 0	+ 4	+ 7	+ 9

4 Circle the answer in each of the questions below.

a The 3 in 359 is in the	ones place	tens place	hundreds place
b The 4 in 904 is in the	ones place	tens place	hundreds place
c The 5 in 256 is in the	ones place	tens place	hundreds place

(continued on next page)

NAME _____ | DATE _____

Numbers, Cubes & Marbles page 2 of 2

5 Ebony put 10 cubes into two stacks. One stack has 4 more cubes than the other stack.

a How many cubes are in each stack? Show your work.

There are _____ cubes in one stack and _____ cubes in the other stack.

b Which strategy did you use to solve this problem? (Circle one.)

Draw a picture   Act it out with cubes   Make a list   Other

6 **CHALLENGE** Jose has a bag of marbles. There are 8 red marbles in the bag. There are twice as many green marbles as red marbles. There are 2 fewer blue marbles than green marbles. There are half as many white marbles as blue marbles.

a How many marbles are in the bag? Show your work.

There are _____ marbles in the bag.

b Which strategy did you use to solve this problem? (Circle one.)

Draw a picture   Act it out with cubes   Make a list   Other

NAME _____ | **DATE** _____

🏠 Place Value on Wheels page 1 of 2

1 Read each number. Then write it in expanded form.

ex fifty-six $56 = 50 + 6$	**a** thirty-two	**b** seventy-five
c eighteen	**d** seventy-four	**e** twenty-eight
f ninety-three	**g** forty-five	**h** sixty-seven

2 Find each sum.

$60 + 8 =$ _____ $20 + 3 =$ _____ $50 + 9 =$ _____

$70 + 15 =$ _____ $40 + 17 =$ _____ $10 + 18 =$ _____

$60 + 14 =$ _____ $50 + 13 =$ _____ $50 + 19 =$ _____

$$\begin{array}{c} 30 \\ + 19 \\ \hline \end{array} \qquad \begin{array}{c} 60 \\ + 16 \\ \hline \end{array} \qquad \begin{array}{c} 20 \\ + 17 \\ \hline \end{array} \qquad \begin{array}{c} 40 \\ + 14 \\ \hline \end{array} \qquad \begin{array}{c} 80 \\ + 11 \\ \hline \end{array} \qquad \begin{array}{c} 40 \\ + 15 \\ \hline \end{array} \qquad \begin{array}{c} 70 \\ + 12 \\ \hline \end{array}$$

3 Circle the correct answer.

a The 5 in 581 is in the	ones place	tens place	hundreds place
b The 5 in 358 is in the	ones place	tens place	hundreds place
c The 5 in 205 is in the	ones place	tens place	hundreds place
d The 5 in 502 is in the	ones place	tens place	hundreds place

(continued on next page)

🏠 **129**

NAME _____ | DATE _____

Place Value on Wheels page 2 of 2

4 There are 10 bikes and 6 cars in the school parking lot. How many wheels in all? Show your work.

There are _____ wheels in the parking lot.

5 **CHALLENGE** Ben saw some wagons and trikes on the playground. In all, he saw 27 wheels. How many wagons and how many trikes did he see? There are two possible answers. Can you find both of them? Show your work.

_____ wagons and _____ trikes	_____ wagons and _____ trikes

NAME _____ | **DATE** _____

 Last Shape In Wins page 1 of 2

Note to Families

Last Shape In Wins is an easy and fun strategy game that gives children a chance to see the results of combining some familiar shapes. We play it at school with pattern blocks, but you'll be coloring in the shapes instead. Have fun!

Materials

- Last Shape In Wins, pages 1–2
- crayons, markers, or colored pencils in the following colors: yellow, green, blue, and red

Instructions

1 With your partner, decide who will go first and who will go second.

2 Take turns coloring in shapes on the first game board.

    a You may color in one or more triangles to form one of the shapes shown below.

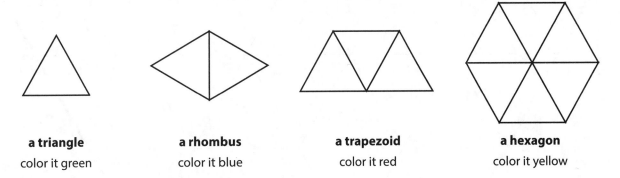

| **a triangle** | **a rhombus** | **a trapezoid** | **a hexagon** |
| color it green | color it blue | color it red | color it yellow |

    b You can color in any one of the four shapes anywhere on the game board each time it's your turn. It is a good idea to outline the shape first before you start coloring.

    c You must take your turn every time.

3 The winner is the player who gets to complete filling in the game board (the big hexagon) by coloring in the last shape.

4 **CHALLENGE** Try to use the fewest number of shapes to fill in the big hexagon. See if you can use even fewer the second time you play.

5 When you have time, play the game a second time.

(continued on next page)

NAME | DATE

Last Shape In Wins page 2 of 2

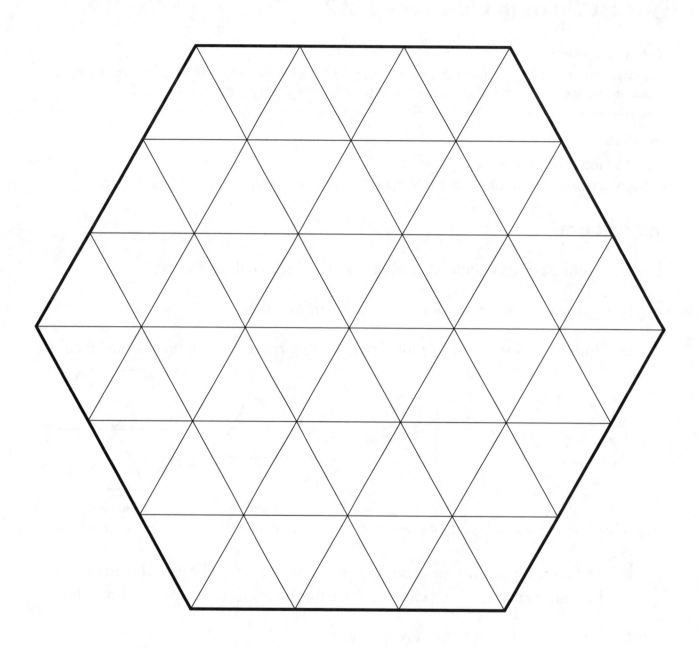

Shapes

a triangle
color it green

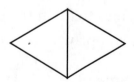

a rhombus
color it blue

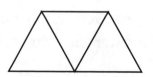

a trapezoid
color it red

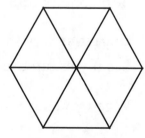

a hexagon
color it yellow

NAME _____ **| DATE** _____

 Facts & Shapes page 1 of 2

1 Match each Unifix train to its fact family triangle. Then write 2 addition and 2 subtraction equations to match. Write them under the train.

ex

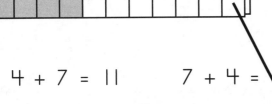

$$4 + 7 = 11 \qquad 7 + 4 = 11$$
$$11 - 4 = 7 \qquad 11 - 7 = 4$$

a

b

c

d

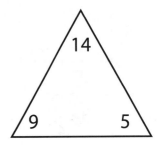

14
9   5

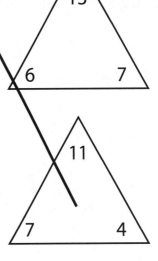

13
6   7

11
7   4

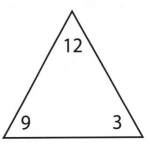

12
9   3

13
8   5

(continued on next page)

Facts & Shapes page 2 of 2

2 Count the money to find out how much each shape is worth. Write the price on the shape.

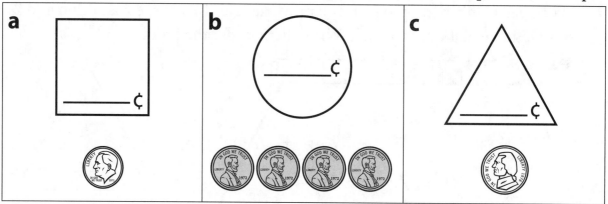

3 Maria bought some shapes at the Shapes Shop. She used all her shapes to make this picture. How much money did she spend? Show your work.

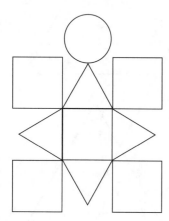

4 Use squares, circles, and triangles to make a picture worth 48¢. Label your work to prove it.

Sorting Quadrilaterals page 1 of 2

Note to Families

This Home Connection Activity involves sorting quadrilaterals. Although some of these shapes are pretty strange-looking, they're all related in that they each have 4 sides and 4 corners. Your child may have many different ideas about how to sort the quadrilaterals on the next page, but if he or she runs out of steam, it's okay for you to mention things like right angles, parallel lines, and symmetry. Have fun!

Cut out the shape cards on the next page. Some of the shapes may look a little strange to you, but they are all quadrilaterals. That is, they all have 4 sides. Look carefully and you'll find that it's true! Work with someone in your family to find as many ways to sort these shapes as possible, and list your ideas below.

"These all have at least 1 line of symmetry."   "None of these are symmetrical."

symmetrical   not symmetrical

NAME | **DATE**

Sorting Quadrilaterals page 2 of 2

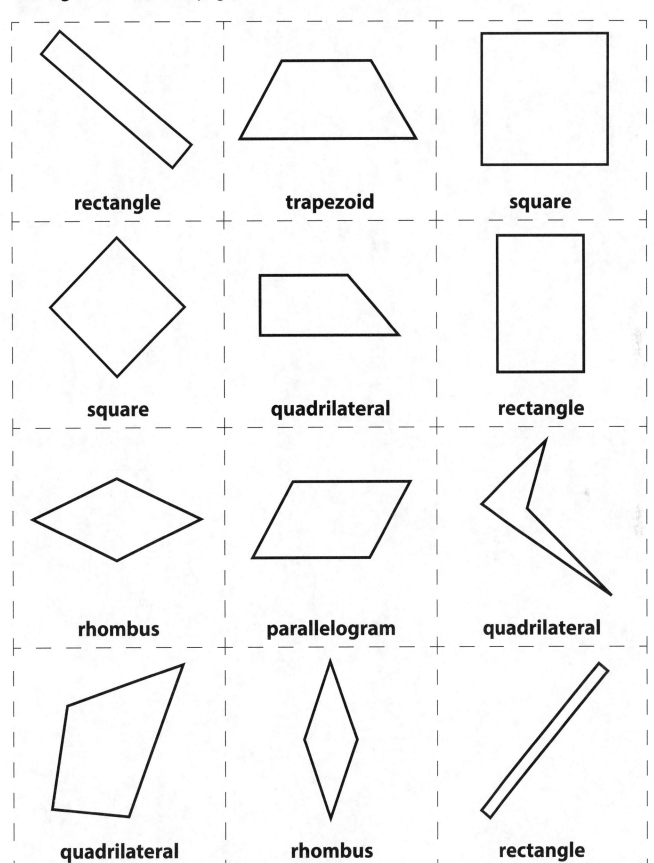

rectangle   **trapezoid**   **square**

square   **quadrilateral**   **rectangle**

rhombus   **parallelogram**   **quadrilateral**

quadrilateral   **rhombus**   **rectangle**

NAME _____ | DATE _____

 Three-Dimensional Shape Hunt page 1 of 2

Note to Families

We recently started a new unit on geometry. We are using pattern blocks, geoboards, and paper shapes to investigate many different two- and three-dimensional shapes. Besides learning to recognize and name these shapes, we'll explore how they're alike and different and what happens when we cut them up, put them together, and move them around by sliding, turning, and flipping them. We'll learn how to measure the area of some of them, and how to use others to create symmetrical designs. We'll also consider the shapes that are all around us, both human-made and those occuring in nature. This assignment reinforces what we are learning about geometry.

Have you ever thought about why things are the shape they are? Ever wondered why a cup is round and the rooms in most houses are square or rectangular instead of round? Why dice and ice are cube-shaped and why we eat ice cream out of cones instead of pyramids? Shapes are fun to find and fun to think about! This week, you're going to go on a three-dimensional shape hunt. All you have to do is search around your house for things that are shaped like cubes, spheres, cylinders, and rectangular prisms (boxes), and list them below. Happy hunting!

Here are some of things we found that are cylindrical:

Here are some of things we found that are spherical:

Here are some of the things we found that are shaped like rectangular prisms:

Here are some of the things we found that are shaped like cubes:

(continued on next page)

NAME _____ | **DATE** _____

Three-Dimensional Shape Hunt page 2 of 2

Note to Families

This exercise asks your child to count and sketch the faces of two different three-dimensional shapes. "Face" is the term mathematicians use for a flat surface on a three-dimensional shape. The triangular prism pictured to the left has 5 faces: 2 triangles and 3 rectangles. Your child will need a cube and a rectangular prism to do this exercise. One of a pair of dice and a cereal box would be great.

Materials

- Three-Dimensional Shape Hunt, page 2
- a cube, such as one of a pair of dice
- a rectangular prism, such as a cereal box

Instructions

Take a good look at some of the shapes you found to answer the following questions.

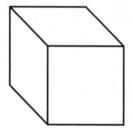

How many faces does your cube have? _____

Are they all the same shape? _____

Make a sketch of each of the cube's faces right here:

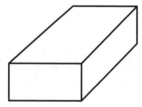

How many faces does your rectangular prism have? _____

What shape(s) are they? _____

Please sketch each of the rectangular prism's faces here:

NAME _____ | **DATE** _____

 Missing Numbers page 1 of 2

1 One number from each family is lost! Write the missing number in the triangle. Use the pictures to help. Then write 2 addition and 2 subtraction equations to match.

ex
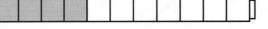

$5 + 7 = 12$ $12 - 5 = 7$

$7 + 5 = 12$ $12 - 7 = 5$

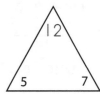

a
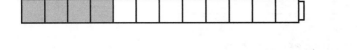

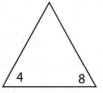

b
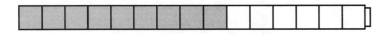

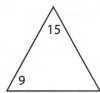

c
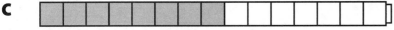

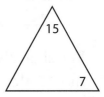

2 Fill in the missing numbers to solve these equations.

$6 + 7 + 3 = $ _____ $8 + 1 + $ _____ $ = 18$ $5 + $ _____ $ + 2 = 13$

$13 - $ _____ $ = 8$ $12 - $ _____ $ = 7$ $12 - 4 = $ _____

3 **CHALLENGE** Fill in the missing numbers to solve these equations.

$40 + 18 + 23 = $ _____ $60 + 47 + $ _____ $ = 126$ _____ $ + 67 + 26 = 131$

(continued on next page)

NAME _____ | **DATE** _____

Missing Numbers page 2 of 2

4 Draw a line to match each problem with its equation. Then find the answers.

a The pet shop owner had 14 hamsters. She sold 5 of them on Monday and 3 of them on Tuesday. How many hamsters does she have left?	$9 - 2 + 8 =$ _____
b There were 12 puppies in the pen. The pet shop owner sold some of them. Now there are 7 puppies in the pen. How many puppies did she sell?	$14 - 5 - 3 =$ _____
c The pet shop owner got 9 rabbits yesterday. A family came in and bought 2 of them. Then the shop owner got 8 more rabbits. How many rabbits does she have now?	$6 +$ _____ $= 13$
d There were 16 fish in the big tank. The shop owner moved some of them. Now there are only 9 fish in the big tank. How many did the shop owner move?	$12 -$ _____ $= 7$
e The shop owner had 6 kittens. Then she got some more kittens. Now she has 13 kittens. How many kittens did she get?	$16 -$ _____ $= 9$

5 **CHALLENGE** Solve these equations.

$2 + 5 - 4 + 8 =$ _____ $8 + 12 + 34 =$ _____ $20 + 30 -$ _____ $= 30 - 5$

$90 + 170 + 64 =$ _____ $30 - 20 +$ _____ $= 25$ $123 + 48 -$ _____ $= 123 - 5$

_____ $+ 5 = 21$ $250 + 48 + 2 =$ _____ $350 + 118 + 6 =$ _____

🏠 Halves, Bowls & Vans page 1 of 2

1 Circle the correct answer.

a If you cut this square in half, what two shapes will you get?

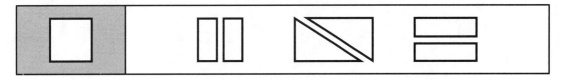

b If you cut this rectangle in half, what two shapes will you get?

c If you cut this hexagon in half, what two shapes will you get?

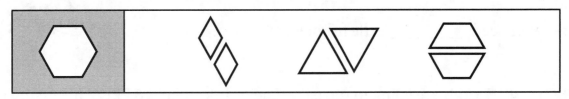

2 Find each difference.

10	16	20	12	14	18	6
− 5	− 8	− 10	− 6	− 7	− 9	− 3

40	60	24	30	80	100	22
− 20	− 30	− 12	− 15	− 40	− 50	− 11

400	600	200	120	180	160	140
− 200	− 300	− 100	− 60	− 90	− 80	− 70

(continued on next page)

Halves, Bowls & Vans page 2 of 2

3 Josh got 12 goldfish. He wants to put 3 goldfish in each little fishbowl. How many little fishbowls will he need? Show your work.

Josh will need _____ little fishbowls.

4 <u>CHALLENGE</u> 36 kids are going to the park. Each van can hold 6 kids. How many vans will they need to take all the kids to the park? Show your work.

They will need _____ vans to take all the kids to the park.

144

NAME | **DATE**

 Half & Half page 1 of 2

1 Circle the shape in each box that has been divided in half.

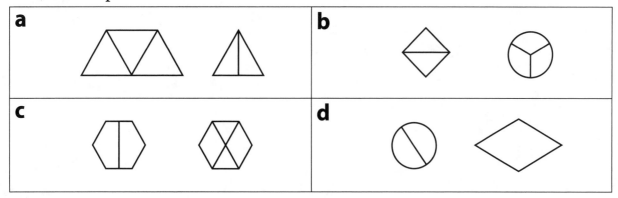

2 Circle the shapes that show two halves. Then color in half of each of them.

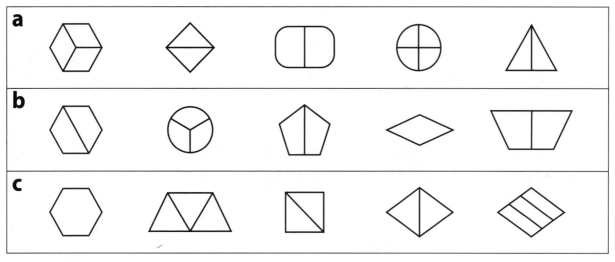

3 Color $\frac{1}{2}$ of the objects in each box.

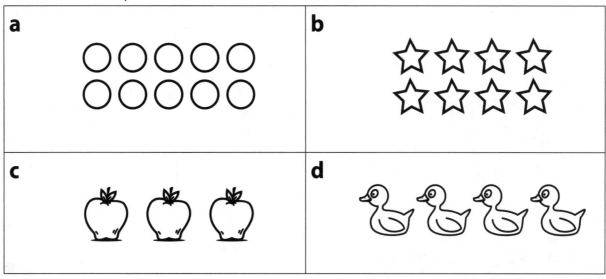

(continued on next page)

Half & Half page 2 of 2

4 Rob had 16 shells. He gave half of them to his brother. How many shells does Rob have now? Show your work.

Rob has _____ shells now.

5 Jess had 28 marbles. She gave half of them to Eli. Then Jess gave half of the marbles she had left to her sister. How many marbles does Jess have now? Show your work.

Jess has _____ marbles now.

Halves & Extra Facts page 1 of 2

Cutting Numbers in Half

1 Since we've been talking about halves, let's see what happens when we "cut" some numbers in half.

What's half of 2?	What's half of 6?	What's half of 10?
What's half of 20?	What's half of 60?	What's half of 100?
What's half of 200?	What's half of 600?	What's half of 1,000?

2 What makes it pretty easy to divide these numbers in half?

3 Solve these half facts.

10	100	8	80	12	120	40
− 5	− 50	− 4	− 40	− 6	− 60	− 20

14	18	16	20	6	60	200
− 7	− 9	− 8	− 10	− 3	− 30	− 100

4 Now try these subtraction combinations.

12	13	12	16	15	16	16
− 6	− 6	− 7	− 8	− 8	− 9	− 7

(continued on next page)

Halves & Extra Facts page 2 of 2

Sometimes story problems give you more facts than you need to solve the problem. In each problem below, cross out the fact you don't need. Then solve the problem. Show your work.

5 Jenny has 12 toy people. She is building a house for them. She used 12 blocks for the front gate and 48 blocks for the rest of the house. How many blocks did Jenny use in all?

Jenny used _____ blocks in all.

6 Juan had 56 crayons. He gave 23 of his crayons to his friend. Juan also gave his friend 15 marking pens. How many crayons does Juan have left?

Juan has _____ crayons left.

7 **CHALLENGE** The Toy Factory made 90 robots on Tuesday. There are 23 workers at the factory. They sold 54 of the robots on Wednesday. How many robots did they have left?

The Toy Factory had _____ robots left.

148

NAME _____ | **DATE** _____

 Exploring Symmetry page 1 of 2

1 Look at the shapes below.

   a Circle the shapes that are symmetrical.

   b Cross out the shapes that are not symmetical.

Square	Circle	Scalene Triangle	Rectangle
Pentagon	Ellipse	Right Triangle	Trapezoid

2 What is the name of each shape, and how many lines of symmetry does it have? Write the name of each shape on the line. Then use your ruler and a pencil to draw in the lines of symmetry, and write the number on the line below the shape name.

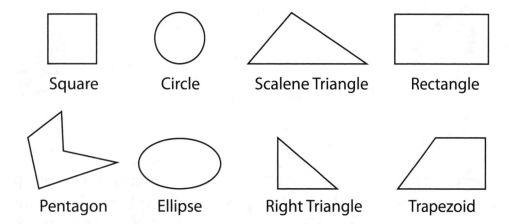

ex

This is an equilateral triangle.

It has   3   line(s) of symmetry.

a

This is a _____

It has _____ line(s) of symmetry.

b

This is a _____

It has _____ line(s) of symmetry.

c

This is a _____

It has _____ line(s) of symmetry.

(continued on next page)

NAME | **DATE**

Exploring Symmetry page 2 of 2

3 Draw the other half of each of these figures as carefully as you can so they're symmetrical when you're finished. (Hint: If you want to see what the whole figure looks like before you draw the other half, set a mirror upright down the midline and take a peek.)

4 Now, here comes the fun part. Have someone in your family draw half a picture of something symmetrical, like a pair of glasses, or a teddy bear, or a butterfly, or…. Then take your pencil and crayons and draw in the other half. When you're finished, you draw a half picture and let a family member draw in the other half.

150

NAME _____ | DATE _____

 Different Ways to Look at the Same Number page 1 of 2

1 Use the pictures to help fill in the answers below.

a Sara built 300 with hundreds mats.

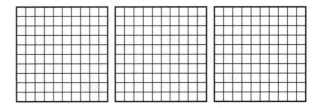

There are _____ 100s in 300.

b Her brother traded in each mat for 10 strips of tens.

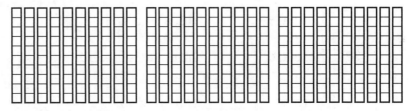

There are _____ 10s in 300.

c If you traded in all the strips for units of one, how many 1s would that be?

There are _____ 1s in 300.

2 Check to make sure there are really 300 units. Loop groups of 10s in different colors. Then label the groups of 10. (10, 20, 30, …)

(continued on next page)

151

Different Ways to Look at the Same Number page 2 of 2

3 Tell how many hundreds, tens, and ones there are in each number. Use the pictures to help.

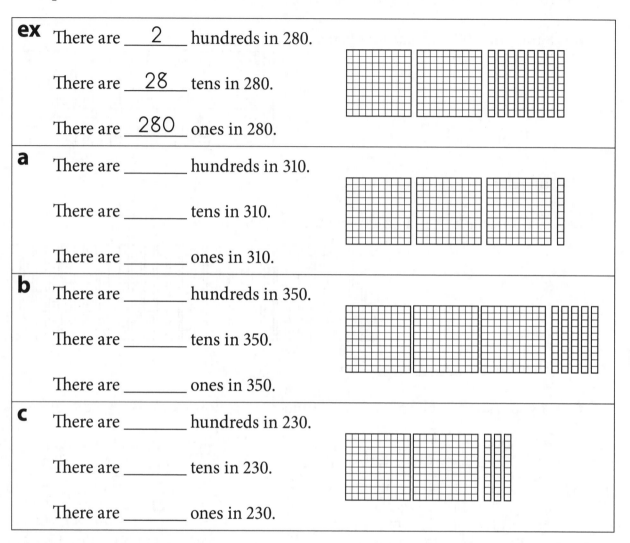

ex There are ___2___ hundreds in 280.

There are ___28___ tens in 280.

There are ___280___ ones in 280.

a There are _____ hundreds in 310.

There are _____ tens in 310.

There are _____ ones in 310.

b There are _____ hundreds in 350.

There are _____ tens in 350.

There are _____ ones in 350.

c There are _____ hundreds in 230.

There are _____ tens in 230.

There are _____ ones in 230.

4 **CHALLENGE** Draw a line from the number on the left to its matching number on the right.

5 hundreds + 2 tens + 9 ones	420 ones
42 tens	52 tens + 9 ones
30 tens + 9 ones	12 tens + 9 ones
1 hundred + 20 tens + 9 ones	3 hundreds + 9 ones

NAME _____ | DATE _____

 Ants & Hotdogs page 1 of 2

1 How many centimeters does the army ant have to go to get to each bug? Use the centimeter side of your ruler to find out.

   a On Path A the army ant has to travel _____ centimeters.

   b On Path B the army ant has to travel _____ centimeters.

   c On Path C the army ant has to travel _____ centimeters.

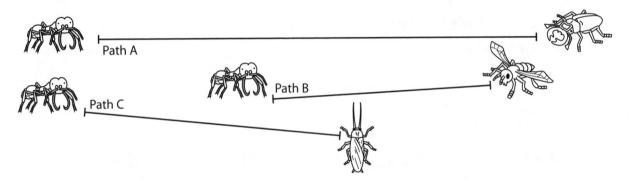

2 The army ants want to get the scorpion. They can use Path A, B, or C.

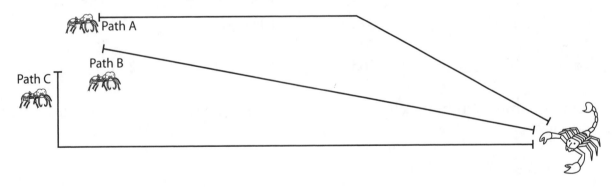

   a Use the centimeter side of your ruler to measure each path. Write each length on the lines below.

     Path A _____   Path B _____   Path C _____

   b If you were an army ant, which path would you use? Path _____
     Why?

(continued on next page)

NAME _____ | DATE _____

Ants & Hotdogs page 2 of 2

3 Sam has a hot dog stand at the mall. The chart below shows how many hot dogs he sold last week. Use the chart to help answer the questions below.

a Which day did Sam sell the most hot dogs?

b Which day did Sam sell the fewest hot dogs?

c How many hot dogs did Sam sell on Tuesday and Wednesday put together? Show your work.

Hot Dogs Sold	
Day	**Number of Hot Dogs**
Monday	119
Tuesday	125
Wednesday	163
Thursday	108
Friday	234
Saturday	345
Sunday	325

4 Use one of the signs below to compare the number of hot dogs Sam sold on different days.

$<$ less than $=$ equal to $>$ greater than

125 ___ $<$ ___ 345   325 _____ 108   108 _____ 119

234 _____ 164   163 _____ 345   325 _____ 234

5 Put the numbers from the chart (in problem 3) in order from least to greatest on the lines below.

_____, _____, _____, _____, _____, _____, _____
least   greatest

6 CHALLENGE How many hot dogs did Sam sell in all? Show your work.

Subtraction & Measuring Practice page 1 of 2

DJ likes to make hops on the number line to solve 2-digit subtraction problems, like this:

54 – 25

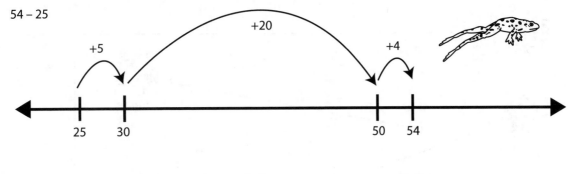

$5 + 20 + 4 = 29$ so 54 – 25 = $\underline{29}$

1 Solve each of the subtraction problems below. You can use DJ's number line strategy or some other way to solve the problem. Show your work each time.

a 56 – 29

_____ so 56 – 29 = _____

b 70 – 36

_____ so 70 – 36 = _____

c 63 – 19

_____ so 63 – 19 = _____

(continued on next page)

NAME _____ | **DATE** _____

Subtraction & Measuring Practice page 2 of 2

2 Measure the ladybugs' paths below. Use the centimeter side of your ruler. Write the length of each path on the correct line.

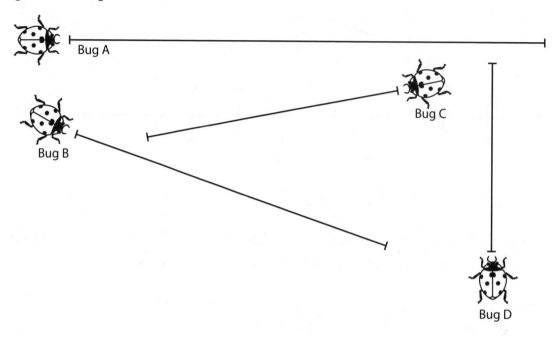

Bug A walked _____ cm   Bug B walked _____ cm

Bug C walked _____ cm   Bug D walked _____ cm

3 Which ladybug has the longest path? (circle one)

Bug A   Bug B   Bug C   Bug D

4 How much longer is Bug A's path than Bug B's path? _____

5 How much shorter is Bug D's path than Bug A's path? _____

6 How far did the 4 ladybugs walk in all? Write an equation to show.

7 Draw a path from the ladybug to the flower. Measure it with the centimeter side of your ruler.

My path is _____ centimeters long.

NAME _____ | **DATE** _____

 More Ant Stories page 1 of 2

1 There are 4 lines of ants. There are 5 ants in every line. The queen wants 30 ants for her parade.

a How many ants are lined up right now? Show your work.

b How many more ants need to line up? Show your work.

2 **CHALLENGE** Use the numbers in the box to fill in the blanks below.

18	11	3	5
	23	16	10
6	12	4	17

a Find 2 numbers whose sum is 21. _____, _____

b Find 2 numbers whose sum is 29. _____, _____

c Find 2 numbers whose difference is 10. _____, _____

d Find 2 numbers whose difference is 14. _____, _____

e Find 4 numbers that have the smallest total. _____, _____, _____, _____

(continued on next page)

NAME | **DATE**

More Ant Stories page 2 of 2

Hi! I am a worker army ant. I am 1 centimeter long.

My 10 army ant friends make a line that is 10 centimeters, or 1 decimeter, long.

3 List four different things on you or in your kitchen that are about the same length as a decimeter.

4 Use your ruler to help draw a line below that is exactly 15 centimeters long. How many of us army ants could stand on your line?

5 One hundred of my army ant friends would make a line that is 100 centimeters, or 1 meter long. That's about the same as the distance between the floor and the doorknob on a regular door.

List four different things in your home that are about the same length as a meter.

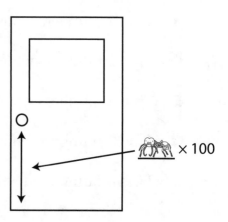

× 100

NAME   **| DATE**

 Fraction Races & More page 1 of 2

Note to Families

Here are the rules for a new fraction game we learned in school. Please play this game with your child several times. Then have your child complete the exercise on the back of this sheet and return it to school.

---

1   Use the extra set of construction paper strips to fold, cut, and label another fraction kit. It should be just like the one you brought home with you.

2   Set your whole strip out in front of you and stack the other fraction pieces to the side so you're ready to play. Have your partner do the same.

3   Anchor a paperclip with a pencil and use it as a spinner arrow. Spin the spinner and take the fraction piece that it names and lay it on top of your whole strip. Then give your partner a turn. Continue taking turns back and forth until one of you has filled your whole strip. The tricky part is that you have to go out evenly. If you spin a fourth and then a half, so that three-fourths of your whole strip is covered, and then spin another half, you can't use it. In this case, you lose your turn and have to wait until your next turn to try again.

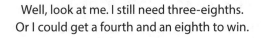

| Oh no! I have a fourth left to go and I just spun a half! I can't use it. What I need is a fourth or an eighth. | Well, look at me. I still need three-eighths. Or I could get a fourth and an eighth to win. |

4   When one person has won by filling his or her entire strip with fraction pieces, clear them off and play again.

5   When this seems easy, play backward. That is, start by covering your whole strip with fraction pieces. (You can do this using any combination of pieces you want—2 halves, 4 fourths, a half, a fourth, and 2 eighths, etc. You may have to do some trading along the way.) Then take turns spinning the spinner and removing the pieces it names. The first person to remove all of his or her pieces from the strip is the winner.

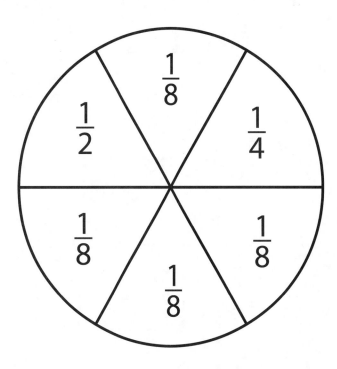

(continued on next page)

NAME | DATE

Fraction Races & More page 2 of 2

Comparing Fractions

Use your fraction pieces to do the exercises below.

1 Circle the larger of the two fractions in each pair. The first one is done for you.

ex

$\frac{2}{8}$ $\left(\frac{3}{4}\right)$

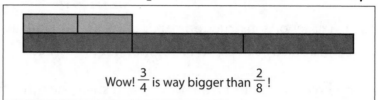

Wow! $\frac{3}{4}$ is way bigger than $\frac{2}{8}$!

a $\frac{1}{2}$ $\frac{1}{4}$ **b** $\frac{1}{4}$ $\frac{3}{8}$ **c** $\frac{3}{8}$ $\frac{1}{2}$

2 Circle the smaller of the two fractions in each pair.

a $\frac{1}{8}$ $\frac{1}{4}$ **b** $\frac{1}{4}$ $\frac{3}{8}$ **c** $\frac{3}{8}$ $\frac{1}{2}$

3 Lay out each combination of fractions shown below and find one fraction piece that is the same length. The first one is done for you.

ex

$\frac{1}{8} + \frac{1}{8} = \underline{\quad \frac{1}{4} \quad}$

Well, that's pretty easy. If I lay 2 eighths end to end, I can see that the one-fourth piece is exactly the same length.

a $\frac{1}{4} + \frac{1}{4} = \underline{\qquad}$ **b** $\frac{1}{2} + \frac{1}{2} = \underline{\qquad}$

c $\frac{2}{8} + \frac{1}{4} = \underline{\qquad}$ **d** $\frac{1}{4} + \frac{1}{4} + \frac{1}{4} + \frac{1}{4} = \underline{\qquad}$

e $\frac{1}{4} + \frac{1}{4} + \frac{1}{2} = \underline{\qquad}$ **f** $\frac{1}{8} + \frac{1}{8} + \frac{1}{4} = \underline{\qquad}$

160

Twice as Big? page 1 of 3

Note To Families

This Home Connection activity will give your child an opportunity to measure and compare length and circumference in centimeters. If you don't have a cloth centimeter tape measure at home, you'll need to cut and tape the paper strips on the next page together to make one. Although this won't be the sturdiest measuring device in the world, it will probably hold together long enough to complete this activity.

Many kids your age think that they're probably about half as big as the adults in their family. Do you think this is true for you? Let's do some measuring and find out. First, you'll need to find a cloth centimeter tape measure around your house, or tape the paper strips on page 3 together to make one. Now you're all set! Use your tape measure to help answer the following questions:

1 How long is your hand and forearm, from the tip of your middle finger to your elbow? _____ cm

2 How long is the adult's hand and forearm? _____ cm

3 How much longer is the adult's hand and forearm than yours? _____ cm

4 Circle the words that make this a true sentence:
The adult's hand and forearm is _____ the length of mine.

       exactly twice   more than twice   less than twice

5 How big around is your wrist? _____ cm

6 How big around is the adult's wrist? _____ cm

7 How much bigger around is the adult's wrist than yours? _____ cm

(continued on next page)

161

NAME _____ | DATE _____

Twice as Big? page 2 of 3

8 Circle the words that make this a true sentence:

The adult's wrist is _____ big around as mine.

exactly twice   more than twice   less than twice

9 How long is your foot? _____ cm

10 How long is the adult's foot? _____ cm

11 How much longer is the adult's foot than yours? _____ cm

12 Circle the words that make this a true sentence:

The adult's foot is _____ as big as mine.

exactly twice   more than twice   less than twice

13 Now, see if you can find one measurement on the adult that is very close to twice as big as the same measurement on you.

The adult's _____ is about twice the length/circumference as mine.

14 Would you say, overall, that the adult is _____ as big as you?
- ○ more than twice
- ○ less than twice
- ○ about twice

162

Twice as Big? page 3 of 3

	glue or tape	glue or tape	glue or tape	glue or tape
1	21	41	61	81
2	22	42	62	82
3	23	43	63	83
4	24	44	64	84
5	25	45	65	85
6	26	46	66	86
7	27	47	67	87
8	28	48	68	88
9	29	49	69	89
10	30	50	70	90
11	31	51	71	91
12	32	52	72	92
13	33	53	73	93
14	34	54	74	94
15	35	55	75	95
16	36	56	76	96
17	37	57	77	97
18	38	58	78	98
19	39	59	79	99
20	40	60	80	100

NAME _____ **|DATE** _____

 Numbers & Buttons page 1 of 2

1 Read each number. Then write it in expanded form.

ex four hundred fifteen 415 = 400 + 10 + 5	**a** two hundred eighty-six
b seven hundred fifty-three	**c** six hundred twenty-one
d three hundred forty-seven	**e** nine hundred seventeen
f one hundred sixty	**g** eight hundred four

2 Find each sum.

500 + 20 + 8 = _____   200 + 20 + 2 = _____   100 + 70 + 1 = _____

700 + 10 + 9 = _____   800 + 40 + 7 = _____   500 + 3 = _____

$$\begin{array}{r} 200 \\ 90 \\ +\,1 \\ \hline \end{array} \qquad \begin{array}{r} 300 \\ 10 \\ +\,9 \\ \hline \end{array} \qquad \begin{array}{r} 200 \\ 20 \\ +\,6 \\ \hline \end{array} \qquad \begin{array}{r} 400 \\ 50 \\ +\,2 \\ \hline \end{array} \qquad \begin{array}{r} 900 \\ 90 \\ +\,9 \\ \hline \end{array} \qquad \begin{array}{r} 300 \\ 40 \\ +\,1 \\ \hline \end{array} \qquad \begin{array}{r} 400 \\ 10 \\ +\,8 \\ \hline \end{array}$$

3 Circle the number that has the same value as the expanded form.

a 300 + 6

36   336   306   316

b 200 + 10 + 7

207   217   271   721

(continued on next page)

Numbers & Buttons page 2 of 2

Dylan's grandma has a box of buttons. One day Dylan sorted the buttons into different groups and counted how many in each group. He made a chart to show his work.

4 Help Dylan make a bar graph to show his work. Give the graph a title and color in the columns to show how many buttons of each color he found.

Kind of Button		How Many
⊚	Red	14
◉	Gold	25
◇	White	26
◉	Blue	10
🦪	Purple	5
◉	Black	22

Graph Title _Kinds of Button_

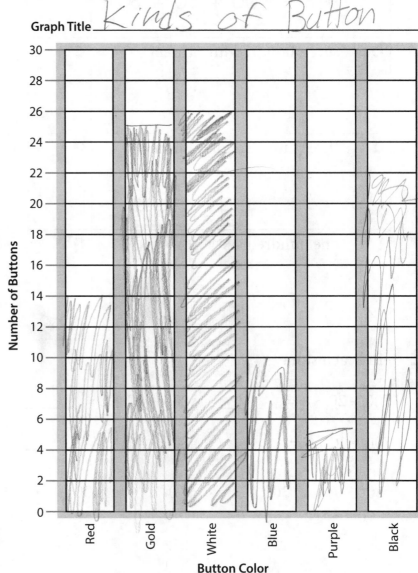

5 How many buttons were in the box in all? Show your work.

$$
\begin{array}{r}
14 \\
25 \\
+26 \\
+10 \\
+5 \\
+22 \\
\hline
102
\end{array}
$$

There were _102_ buttons in the box in all.

Fractions & Money page 1 of 2

1 What part of each rectangle is colored? Circle the correct fraction.

a

$\frac{1}{3}$ $\frac{2}{2}$ $\frac{1}{2}$ $\frac{3}{4}$

b

$\frac{1}{4}$ $\frac{2}{4}$ $\frac{1}{3}$ $\frac{3}{6}$

c

$\frac{2}{3}$ $\frac{1}{2}$ $\frac{3}{4}$ $\frac{1}{3}$

d

$\frac{3}{4}$ $\frac{2}{4}$ $\frac{3}{3}$ $\frac{5}{4}$

2 Read each fraction and color in that part of the shape.

a

two-fourths $\frac{2}{4}$

b

three-fourths $\frac{3}{4}$

c

one-third $\frac{1}{3}$

d

three-thirds $\frac{3}{3}$

(continued on next page)

Fractions & Money page 2 of 2

3 Breanna has a pair of shorts with 4 pockets. She has money in each pocket. Finish the chart below to see how much.

Pocket	Quarters	Dimes	Nickels	Pennies	Total
a	2	2	1	2	77¢
b	1	0	5	9	
c	3	0	1	3	
d	0	4	3	1	

4 In which pocket does Breanna have the most money? _____

5 In which pocket does Breanna have the least money? _____

6 Breanna wants to buy a toy for $3.00. She thinks she has enough money in her pockets. Do you agree? Explain your answer.

7 How much money does Breanna really have in her 4 pockets? Show your work.

8 **CHALLENGE** Breanna bought 3 pencils at the school store. They each cost 29¢. How much money did she have left in her pockets after she paid for the pencils? Show your work.

🏠 Equations & Story Problems page 1 of 2

1 Fill in the missing numbers.

a 15 = _____ + 7

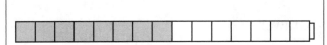

b 5 + _____ = 13

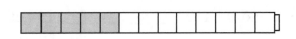

c 14 − _____ = 8

d 16 − _____ = 7

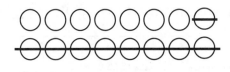

e 9 + 6 = _____ + 8

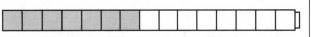

f 12 − 5 = 4 + _____

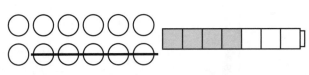

g 13 − 7 = 3 + _____

2 Fill in the missing numbers.

40 + 50 = _____   30 + _____ = 60   _____ + 70 = 90

25 + 35 = _____   25 + _____ = 50   _____ + 40 = 85

80 − 40 = _____   70 − _____ = 20   _____ − 30 = 30

95 − 40 = _____   55 − _____ = 35   _____ − 25 = 25

3 **CHALLENGE** Fill in the missing numbers.

250 = _____ + 6   90 + 70 = _____ + 17   140 − 60 = 30 + _____

(continued on next page)

NAME _____ **| DATE** _____

Equations & Story Problems page 2 of 2

Fill in the blanks with words that make sense and seem interesting. Solve each problem. Show your work.

Fill in the blanks.	Work Space
4 Kendra has 57 _____ in her top drawer. She has 28 _____ in her bottom drawer. How many are there in all? _____	
5 Lin spent 39 dollars for a _____. He spent 18 dollars for a _____. How much did he spend in all? _____	
6 Akiko had 72 _____. She gave 26 of them to her friend. How many does she have left? _____	
7 Mr. Smith baked 48 _____. The dog ate 19 of them. How many are left? _____	
8 Frank saw 51 _____. Then 24 of them flew away. How many were left? _____	

170

NAME _____ | **DATE** _____

 Cleaning Desks & Measuring Lines page 1 of 2

1 Finish the graph on the right. Give it a title. Color in the columns to show what the kids found in their desks.

Number	Extra Things
44	Extra pencils
18	Extra pair of scissors
12	Extra glue sticks
15	Extra erasers
9	Overdue library books

2 How many more pencils than erasers did the kids find? Show your work.

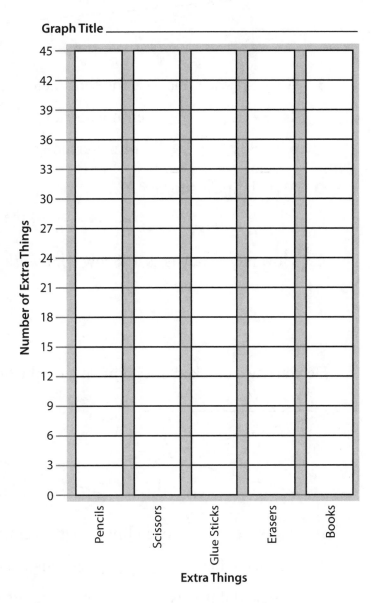

3 **CHALLENGE** How many extra things did they find in all? Show your work.

(continued on next page)

NAME _____ | DATE _____

Cleaning Desks & Measuring Lines page 2 of 2

1 Here are two lines. Put an X on the one you think is shorter.

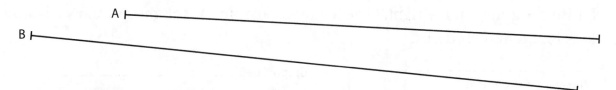

a Measure each line. Use the centimeter side of your ruler.

Line A is _____ centimeters long.

Line B is _____ centimeters long.

b Which line is shorter? (Circle one.)

Line A   Line B

c How much shorter is it? Show your work. Mark the answer clearly.

2 Here are two crooked lines. Put an x on the one you think is longer.

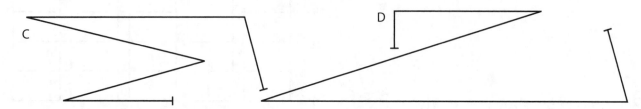

a Measure each crooked line. Use the centimeter side of your ruler.

Crooked line C is _____ centimeters long.

Crooked line D is _____ centimeters long.

b Which crooked line is longer? (Circle one.)

Crooked Line C   Crooked Line D

c How much longer is it? Show your work. Mark the answer clearly.

NAME | DATE

 Estimation Problems page 1 of 2

1 For each problem below, circle the estimate you think is best. On the last two, explain why you chose the estimate you did. Hint: Make your own pictures to help.

Problem & Picture	Estimate	Problem & Picture	Estimate
a 35 + 26	50 60 70	**b** 24 + 24	30 40 50
c 49 + 39	70 80 90	**d** 37 + 24	50 60 70
Why?		Why?	

2 For each problem below, circle the estimate you think is best. On the last two, explain why you chose the estimate you did. Hint: Make your own pictures to help.

Problem & Picture	Estimate	Problem & Picture	Estimate
a 45 − 29	15 20 25	**b** 52 − 18	30 40 50
c 50 − 24	25 30 35	**d** 60 − 29	30 40 50
Why?		Why?	

(continued on next page)

NAME _____ | DATE _____

Estimation Problems page 2 of 2

3 Dora went to the mall yesterday. She got a T-shirt for $9.99 and a new CD for $6.99. About how much money did she spend in all? Circle the estimate you think is best.

$15.00 $16.00 $17.00 $20.00

4 Max got $50.00 for his birthday. He bought 2 video games for $14.00 each. About how much money does he have left? Circle the estimate you think is best.

$10.00 $20.00 $30.00 $40.00

5 Janel is making a quilt. She needs 100 squares of fabric in all. She cut 29 squares this morning and 39 more squares this afternoon. About how many squares does she have left to cut? Circle the estimate you think is best.

10 squares   20 squares   30 squares   40 squares

6 Gerald wants to read 75 books by the end of the year. So far, he has read 18 fantasy books and 21 science books. About how many books does he have left to read? Circle the estimate you think is best.

15 books   25 books   35 books   45 books

7 The second graders at King School are recycling cans.

Day	Number of Cans
Monday	57
Tuesday	98
Wednesday	45
Thursday	105

About how many cans have they recycled so far? Circle the estimate you think is best.

200 cans   300 cans   400 cans   1,000 cans

Riddles & Toys page 1 of 2

1 Tell what digit is in each place.

a 289 _____ is in the tens place.

_____ is in the ones place.

_____ is in the hundreds place.

b 945 _____ is in the ones place.

_____ is in the hundreds place.

_____ is in the tens place.

c 316 _____ is in the tens place.

_____ is in the hundreds place.

_____ is in the ones place.

d 405 _____ is in the ones place.

_____ is in the tens place.

_____ is in the hundreds place.

e 5,687 _____ is in the tens place.

_____ is in the ones place.

_____ is in the thousands place.

_____ is in the hundreds place.

f 4,301 _____ is in the ones place.

_____ is in the hundreds place.

_____ is in the tens place.

_____ is in the thousands place.

2 **CHALLENGE** Solve these number riddles.

I have a 4 in the tens place.

I have a 1 in the hundreds place.

The number in my ones place is more than 6 and less than 9.

I am an odd number.

What number am I? _____

I have a 7 in the hundreds place.

I have a 0 in the tens place.

I have a 3 in the thousands place.

The number in my ones place is less than 3.

I am an even number.

What number am I? _____

(continued on next page)

Riddles & Toys page 2 of 2

Toy Store Price List (prices include tax)

| Doll $8.00 | Skates $29.00 | Puppet $6.00 | Hat $13.00 |

3 Ezra got $50.00 for his birthday. He bought a hat at the toy store. How much money did he have left? Show your work. Mark the answer clearly.

$$\$\cancel{5}\cancel{0}^{10} - 13 = 37$$

$$\begin{array}{r} -13 \\ \hline 37 \end{array}$$

He has $37.00 left.

4 **CHALLENGE** Maya went into the toy store with $50.00. She bought three different toys and got $2.00 back in change. Which three toys did she buy? Show your work. Mark the answer clearly.

NAME _____ | **DATE** _____

 Comparing Numbers & Sharks' Lengths page 1 of 2

1 Circle the place value of the underlined digit. Then write its value.

Number	Place Value	Value	Number	Place Value	Value
ex 2<u>3</u>8	ones / (tens) / hundreds	30	**ex** 10<u>9</u>	(ones) / tens / hundreds	9
a <u>7</u>43	ones / tens / hundreds		**b** 25<u>3</u>	ones / tens / hundreds	
c 1<u>5</u>0	ones / tens / hundreds		**d** <u>6</u>08	ones / tens / hundreds	

2 Write one of these signs on each line to make the equation true.

        < less than   = equal to   > greater than

456 _<_ 546   85 ___ 58   327 ___ 372   106 ___ 610

218 ___ 218   735 ___ 573   204 ___ 240   483 ___ 438

3 Fill in the missing digits to make each equation true. There is more than one right answer for each one.

3_2_7 < 347   235 > ___35   307 < ___07   135 < 13___

4___3 > 463   1___9 < 139   182 > 1___2   514 < 51___

(continued on next page)

NAME _____ |DATE _____

Comparing Numbers & Sharks' Lengths page 2 of 2

There are many different types of sharks. Some are longer than others. This chart shows how long some of the different sharks are. Use it to help answer the questions below.

Shark Lengths

Shark Name	Average Length (in centimeters)*
White Shark	204 centimeters
Bignose Shark	174 centimeters
Night Shark	154 centimeters
Bigeye Thresher	312 centimeters
Tiger Shark	247 centimeters
Thresher Shark	373 centimeters

4 Which shark on the chart is the longest? _____

5 Which shark on the chart is the shortest? _____

6 Write one of these symbols on each blank to make the sentence true.

< less than   = equal to   > greater than

a Length of a Tiger Shark _____ Length of a White Shark

b Length of a Bignose Shark _____ Length of a Tiger Shark

7 Put the lengths of the sharks in order from least to greatest.

_____ , _____ , _____ , _____ , _____ , _____

least   greatest

8 How much longer is a Thresher Shark than a Tiger Shark? Show your work. Mark the answer clearly.

* Source: http://na.nefsc.noaa.gov/sharks/

NAME | DATE

 Meters & Math page 1 of 2

A meter is about the same as the distance between the floor and the doorknob of your front door. Look at your front door, or a meter stick if you have one. Now think about how long 20 meters would be, and answer these questions:

1 If you walked across the biggest room in your home, would you go more or less than 20 meters?

1 meter

2 Is it more or less than 20 meters from your bed to your front door?

3 How long would it take you to run 20 meters? Circle the answer that makes the most sense.

10 seconds   10 minutes   10 hours

4 List at least two different animals that might take 10 minutes to travel 20 meters.

5 Which unit would you use to measure the length of a soccer field? (Circle one.)

centimeters   meters   inches   miles

6 The kids measured the distance across their classroom twice. First, they measured it in centimeters. Then they measured it in meters. Fill in the bubble below the answers they most likely got.

1000 centimeters/10 meters   10 centimeters/1000 meters   100 centimeters/100 meters
            ◯   ◯   ◯

7 **CHALLENGE** The circumference, or distance around, a soccer ball is 68 centimeters. Is that longer or shorter than one meter? By how much? Show your work.

(continued on next page)

NAME | DATE

Meters & Math page 2 of 2

8 Jamal is doing his math homework. He just got 24 for an answer. What was the question? Write down at least three different ideas below.

9 **CHALLENGE** Write at least 10 different equations for 120. You can use addition, subtraction, multiplication, or division.

NAME _____ | DATE _____

🏠 Numbers, Clocks & Crayons page 1 of 2

1 Read each number. Then write it in expanded form.

ex one hundred thirty-eight	**a** three hundred forty-two	**b** two hundred seventy-three
138 = 100 + 30 + 8	342 =	273 =

c two hundred twenty-nine	**d** four hundred sixty-one	**e** six hundred eighteen
229 =	461 =	618 =

f one hundred fifty-seven	**g** nine hundred ninety-nine	**h** eight hundred thirty-five
=	=	=

2 Write the numbers in the box in order on the lines from least to greatest.

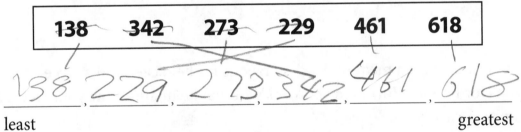

| 138 | 342 | 273 | 229 | 461 | 618 |

138 , 229 , 273 , 342 , 461 , 618

least   greatest

3 Read each of these digital clocks and show the time on the clock face.

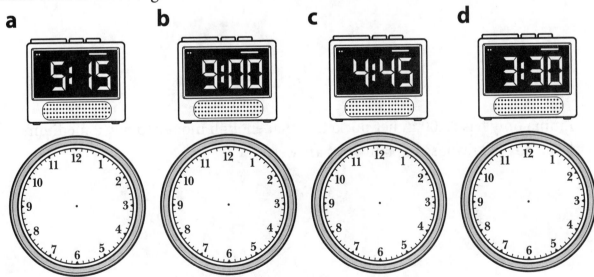

a **5:15**   b **9:00**   c **4:45**   d **3:30**

(continued on next page)

Numbers, Clocks & Crayons page 2 of 2

Small 79¢   Medium 99¢   Large $1.50

You can get boxes of crayons in three different sizes at the store. Use the pictures above to help solve these problems.

4 Miguel bought a small box of crayons. He gave the clerk a $1.00 bill. How much money did he get back? Show your work. Mark the answer clearly.

5 Emma wants to get a medium box of crayons for her sister and a large box of crayons for herself. How many crayons will that be in all? Show your work. Mark the answer clearly.

6 Emma only has $2.00 in her pocket. Is that enough money to buy a medium and a large box of crayons? Explain your answer.

NAME _____ | DATE _____

🏠 Combinations & Crayons page 1 of 2

1 Circle all the combinations that make 100 in red. Then take a pencil and go back and do them. Circle all the combinations that do not make 100 in blue. Then take a pencil and go back and solve them.

70 + 30	60 + 60	20 + 80	75 + 25	50 + 50	100 + 0	50 + 40
60 + 70	96 + 4	95 + 5	70 + 80	60 + 40	93 + 7	0 + 100
100 + 100	10 + 90	40 + 60	25 + 75	92 + 8	20 + 80	100 + 90

2 Add these strings of numbers. Use combinations of 100 to help.

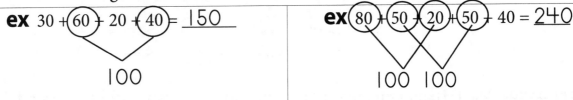

ex 30 + 60 + 20 + 40 = 150 100	**ex** 80 + 50 + 20 + 50 + 40 = 240 100 100
a 30 + 70 + 90 + 10 = _____	**b** 20 + 60 + 40 + 20 = _____
c 90 + 50 + 50 + 30 + 70 = _____	**d** 80 + 20 + 50 + 20 + 50 = _____
e 20 + 98 + 80 + 2 + 43 = _____	**f** 96 + 92 + 4 + 8 + 59 = _____

(continued on next page)

NAME

| DATE

Combinations & Crayons page 2 of 2

Small 79¢   Medium 99¢   Large $1.50

You can get boxes of crayons in 3 different sizes at the store. Use the pictures above to help solve these problems.

3 Sam bought two small boxes of crayons. He gave the clerk $2.00. How much change did he get? Show your work.

4 CHALLENGE Ms. Fernandez bought 10 medium boxes of crayons for her second graders. Then she bought a large box of crayons for herself. She gave the clerk a $20 bill. How much change did she get? Show your work.

Equations, Expressions & Toys page 1 of 2

1 Fill in the missing numbers to solve these addition equations.

50 + 40 + 10 = ___   60 + 4 + ___ = 74   50 + ___ + 9 = 79

80 = 40 + 30 + ___   20 + ___ + 20 = 60   ___ + 30 + 20 = 100

2 Fill in the missing numbers to solve these subtraction equations.

60 − ___ = 40   75 − ___ = 25   120 − 60 = ___

100 − 30 = 20 + ___   90 − 40 = 25 + ___   ___ − 40 = 20 + 30

3 Write a story problem to match this expression. Then solve the problem. Show your work.

83 − 25 =

My Story Problem:

My Work:

(continued on next page)

Equations, Expressions & Toys page 2 of 2

4 Lani has twin brothers. Their birthday is tomorrow. Lani bought a hat for one of the boys and a kite for the other. How much did she spend in all? Show your work.

Lani spent _____ in all.

5 **CHALLENGE** Sam is having a birthday party. Sam's dad bought a kite for each of the children coming to the party. He spent $14.95. How many children did Sam invite? Show your work.

Sam invited _____ children.

NAME _____ | **DATE** _____

 Addition, Subtraction & Fraction Practice page 1 of 2

1 Find each sum.

40	20	57	50	75	34	35
+ 3	+ 38	+ 31	+ 16	+ 25	+ 34	+ 35

290	340	562	225	325	325	450
+ 9	+ 20	+ 35	+ 15	+ 25	+ 26	+ 50

2 Use pictures, numbers, and/or words to add the numbers. Show all your work.

a 47 + 47

b 148 + 122

3 Find each difference.

49	50	67	50	45	30	100
− 9	− 10	− 23	− 25	− 15	− 15	− 75

4 Choose one of the problems in the box. Circle it. Then solve it. Use pictures, numbers, and/or words to help. Show all your work.

35 − 15	50 − 25	83 − 49	123 − 99

(continued on next page)

Addition, Subtraction & Fraction Practice page 2 of 2

5 What part of each set of circles is colored? Circle the correct fraction.

a

$\frac{1}{4}$ $\frac{2}{4}$ $\frac{1}{3}$ $\frac{2}{2}$

b

$\frac{3}{4}$ $\frac{2}{3}$ $\frac{1}{3}$ $\frac{3}{2}$

c

$\frac{3}{4}$ $\frac{4}{3}$ $\frac{1}{3}$ $\frac{4}{4}$

d

$\frac{3}{3}$ $\frac{4}{6}$ $\frac{1}{2}$ $\frac{1}{3}$

6 Follow the directions to complete each picture and then fill in the fraction.

Color $\frac{1}{6}$ of the hexagon yellow.

Color $\frac{2}{6}$ of the hexagon purple.

Color the rest of the hexagon green.

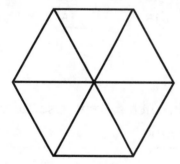

Write a fraction below to show what part of the hexagon is green.

Color $\frac{2}{4}$ of the square red.

Color $\frac{1}{4}$ of the square blue.

Color the rest of the square brown.

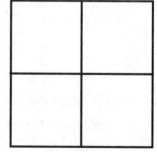

Write a fraction below to show what part of the square is brown.

NAME _____ | DATE _____

 Comparing Animal Weights page 1 of 2

1 Have you ever wondered how much a tiger weighs? Have you ever thought about how heavy a grizzly bear is compared to an alligator? The chart below shows the weights of 7 different animals in kilograms. (A kilogram is a little more than 2 pounds.) Use the information to answer the questions below.

Animal	Weight
Siberian Tiger	230 kilograms
Alligator	270 kilograms
Harbor Seal	170 kilograms
Camel	725 kilograms
Grizzly Bear	680 kilograms
Emperor Penguin	30 kilograms
Gray Wolf	36 kilograms

a Put the weights of these animals in order from least to greatest.

_____ , _____ , _____ , _____ , _____ , _____ , _____

least   greatest

b Which animal on the chart weighs the most? _____

c Which animal on the chart weighs the least? _____

d Which animal weighs more, a Siberian tiger or an alligator?_____

e Which animal weighs less, a grizzly bear or a camel? _____

(continued on next page)

189

NAME | DATE

Comparing Animal Weights page 2 of 2

2 Use numbers, pictures, or words to show how you got the answer.

a Which would weigh more, 3 harbor seals or 2 Siberian tigers?

b Which would weigh less, 5 emperor penguins or 1 harbor seal?

3 Which animal on the chart would you most like to have for a pet? Why?

190

NAME _____ **DATE** _____

🏠 Number Patterns page 1 of 2

1 Fill in the missing numbers in these skip-counting patterns.

a 15, 25, 35, _____, 55, _____, 75, _____, _____, _____, 115, 125

b 6, 12, 18, _____, _____, 36, _____, _____, _____, 60, 66, _____

c 105, 110, 115, _____, _____, 130, _____, _____, 145, _____, 155

d 13, 113, 213, _____, 413 _____, 613, _____, _____, _____

2 DJ and Hopper are jumping from stone to stone to get across the stream. There are 9 stones in all. There is exactly 1 foot between each stone, and there are 12 inches in a foot. Finish the table below to see how many inches the frogs have to jump to get all the way across the stream.

Feet	1	2	3	4	5	6	7	8	9
Inches	12	24			60				

3 **CHALLENGE** The path from DJ's house to the stream is 27 feet long. There are 3 feet in a yard. How many yards is it from DJ's house to the stream? Show your work.

(continued on next page)

NAME _____ | **DATE** _____

Number Patterns page 2 of 2

4 Fill in the missing numbers on the grid below. Use the patterns you know to help.

10	20	30	40	50	60	70	80	90	100
110	120	130	140	150	160	170	180	190	20
210	220	230	240	250	260	270	280	290	300
310	320	330	340	350	360	370	380	390	400
410	420	430	440	460	460	470	480	490	500
510	520		540	550	560	570	580	590	600
610	620	630	640	650	660	670	680	690	700
710	720	730	740	750	760	770	780	790	800
810	820	830	840	850	860	870	880	890	900
910	920		940	950	960	970	980	990	1000

5 Describe at least three different patterns you see on the grid.

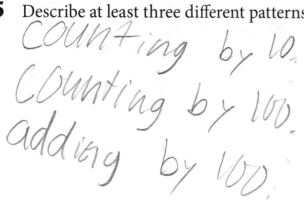

Counting by 10.
Counting by 100.
adding by 100.

Notes

Notes

Notes

Notes